Poetry and Courtliness in Renaissance England

Daniel Javitch

Poetry and Courtliness in Renaissance England

Princeton University Press
Princeton, New Jersey

Copyright © 1978 by Princeton University Press
Published by Princeton University Press, Princeton, New Jersey
In the United Kingdom: Princeton University Press,
Guildford, Surrey
All Rights Reserved
Library of Congress Cataloging in Publication Data will
be found on the last printed page of this book
Publication of this book has been aided by a grant from The
Andrew W. Mellon Foundation
This book has been composed in Linotype Janson
Printed in the United States of America
by Princeton University Press, Princeton, New Jersey

To my Mother and Father

Contents

Acknowledgments

The research and writing of this book were facilitated by several grants from Columbia University's Council for Research in the Humanities and by a summer fellowship from the Henry E. Huntington Library. I am grateful to both institutions for their aid.

A substantial part of Chapter II originally appeared as an article in *Modern Language Notes*, Volume 87 (1972), and I wish to thank the editor, Richard Macksey, for permission to use this material again.

Many friends, students, and colleagues at Columbia University helped me in various ways while I was writing this book. I owe special thanks to J. V. Mirollo and Robert Hanning for their generous advice and encouragement. Leo Braudy, J. A. Mazzeo, William Nelson, J. W. Smit, Joseph Solodow, and Edward Tayler kindly read the manuscript at various stages and made valuable suggestions. Michael Wood gave me some very useful editorial advice after reading a final draft.

I also wish to thank Dante Della Terza, Walter Kaiser, and Harry Levin for their unflagging support of my work. For their patient criticism of my prose I am grateful to David Cheshire, David Detweiler, and Eugene Linden.

Though she disclaims it, I owe my wife Leila the greatest debt.

New York, 1976

Poetry and Courtliness in Renaissance England

Introduction

Social and literary historians of sixteenth-century England have acknowledged that the court, especially Queen Elizabeth's, played a significant role in promoting Tudor poetry. But they simply acknowledge this; they do not, for the most part, explain why the court acted virtually as a nursery of English Renaissance poetry. When general explanations are offered, they tend to be insufficient. For instance, historians maintain that the Tudor court acquired a central role in fostering poetry because the peers, statesmen, and courtiers who were its members assumed the burden of artistic patronage. This is certainly true. Previously, in the Middle Ages, the greatest patrons of English letters and the fine arts had been the sovereign and especially the higher clergy. But the English clergy's economic attrition in the course of the sixteenth century and the tendency of Tudor monarchs to delegate support of the arts to their courtiers meant that the latter became the principal patrons of literature. However, to demonstrate that the patronage of poetry was chiefly aristocratic is still to beg the question: that courtiers lent economic support to poets may attest that they valued and enjoyed poetic entertainment, but it does not provide the reasons for their predilection. Moreover, existing evidence that courtly patronage consisted more of sympathy and of protection than of munificence demands an explanation that goes beyond economic considerations.

What aspects of court life, it must be asked, made the institution so receptive to poetic entertainment? How did the style and behavior cultivated at court stimulate the production of poetry? Such questions have not remained totally unanswered. It is quite often proposed that the enjoyment of sophisticated leisure at court made it a place particularly hospitable to literary entertainment and that Tudor poets could not but benefit from the courtiers' predisposition to play and recreation, especially when, outside the court, influential puritan spokesmen were discrediting poetry as immoral and frivolous. Historians have also observed that the

court's encomiastic needs, the many occasions that called
for praise of the sovereign and other "great" persons, gave
poets special opportunities to display their epideictic skills.
Indeed, this necessity to bestow praise as well as the readi-
ness of princes to have their rules commemorated were as-
pects of court life that stimulated poetic production. So,
in general, did the court's fondness for pageantry and fes-
tive celebration.

Yet useful observations of this sort only begin to suggest
why the late Tudor court fostered poetic talent. The
answer does lie in the social and political nature of courtli-
ness, but exactly why it does remains to be shown. To begin
with, the ways in which the manners cultivated at court
had direct bearing on the welfare of poetry must be illus-
trated more specifically. It is my intent to do so in this book.
More precisely what I seek to show is how poetry benefited
from the code of conduct Elizabethan courtiers espoused.
I want to make clear from the outset that I shall examine
court conduct as it was prescribed rather than as it was
practiced. I believe that during Elizabeth's reign some
courtiers met these prescriptions; I will offer contemporary
evidence that they did; and later in my study I will briefly
speculate about the relationship between the theory and
practice of courtliness. But it is not my intent to consider
actual behavior at Elizabeth's court in any detail. What I
do wish to show is how English poets could gain strength
and status from the ideal of court conduct to which Eliza-
bethans subscribed.

To define this ideal of courtliness I will rely primarily
on Castiglione's *Book of the Courtier*. My dependence on
the Italian book is not arbitrary. *The Courtier* was one of
the most influential conduct books in England. Englishmen
were already reading it in the original soon after it was first
published in 1528. Thomas Hoby's translation appeared in
1561, but it is not until a decade later that the currency of
the book begins to be particularly notable. "All in generall"
the text became, as Hoby had desired, "a storehouse of most
necessarie implements for the conversation, use, and trayn-

ing up of man's life with courtly demeaners." The model
individual depicted in the book represents, in the words of
one important Elizabethan courtier, "the highest and most
perfect type of man."[1] And not only did his fellow courtiers
endorse this ideal, they strove to put it into practice. "How-
ever cynically we may be inclined to reflect that Castiglione
was more honoured in the breach than the observance, it is
more remarkable how closely the profession of courtier,
even in England, adhered to his specification." So concludes
a prominent social historian after studying the conduct and
accomplishments of Elizabeth's principal courtiers.[2] Their
attempts to meet Castiglione's prescriptions of court con-
duct probably helped the Italian code to acquire normative
status. In any case, that it did acquire such status the existing
evidence makes clear. In fact, by relying on the Italian code
to define model norms of late Tudor courtliness, I actually
imitate Elizabethan writers who, instead of formulating
anew the requisites of the English courtier, simply deferred
to Castiglione's prescriptions.[3]

[1] It is Edward Vere, the seventeenth Earl of Oxford (1550-1604),
who maintains that in Castiglione's portrayal of the courtier, "sum-
mum hominem & perfectissimum iudicemus." He makes the com-
ment in his preface to Bartholomew Clerke's Latin translation of the
Cortegiano, first published in London in 1571.

Among the numerous studies that establish the importance and
influence of Castiglione's book in Tudor England see: Walter
Schrinner, *Castiglione und die englische Renaissance* (Berlin, 1939);
Ruth Kelso, *The Doctrine of the English Gentleman in Sixteenth
Century England* (Urbana, Ill., 1929); Caroline Ruutz-Rees, "Some
Notes of Gabriel Harvey's in Hoby's Translation of Castiglione's
Courtier," *PMLA* 25 (1910), 608-639; Daniel Javitch, "Rival Arts of
Conduct in Elizabethan England, Guazzo's *Civile Conversation* and
Castiglione's *Courtier*," *Yearbook of Italian Studies* 1 (1971), 178-198.

[2] A. L. Rowse, *The Elizabethan Renaissance. The Life of the So-
ciety* (London, 1971), p. 56.

[3] So, for example in *Cyvile and Uncyvile Life*, an anonymous dia-
logue on English manners published in 1579, one of the the speakers
refuses to "cumber" his auditor with an account of proper court
conduct. "For to take upon mee," he says, "to frame a Courtier
were presumption, I leave that to the Earle Baldazar, whose Booke
translated by Sir Thomas Hoby, I thinke you have, or ought to

After defining these norms of court conduct, I will demonstrate that they possess marked affinities with poetry. Such affinities, I will argue, proved decisively beneficial for the growth of Elizabethan poetry. First of all, they indicate more precisely why courtiers would be especially sympathetic to poetic art and would offer it opportunities to flourish. These affinities also explain how English poetry improved the precarious status it had throughout the sixteenth century. For poetry's ornamental features, its deceptive verbal tactics, its playful motives—all viewed suspiciously by factions in Tudor society generally hostile to artistic refinement—were bound to gain more respectability by being esteemed at the nation's center of power and fashion. A basic reason why these artifices were so esteemed was their resemblance to the artifices courtiers themselves sought to display in their conduct. Furthermore, because the distinctive features of poetry were so congenial to courtly habits of mind and style, poets or their supporters could accord the art a more important social function than it had been granted. They could rightly maintain that, because its rhetoric agreed with the inclinations of a courtly audience, poetry was more likely to captivate and move those high enough in position to benefit society. At least they could claim that poetry could do so more effectively than other too overtly didactic modes of discourse less compatible with England's governing class. Such a rhetorical advantage helped to enhance the art in the eyes of those many Englishmen who valued discourse only in terms of moral utility; it also served to motivate some of the finest poetic contributions of the age.

The affinities between proper court conduct and the stylistic procedures of poetry can illustrate, I contend, why poetic talent was stimulated and fostered at court. I do not

---

have reade." The text can be found in *Inedited Tracts: illustrating the Manners, Opinions and Occupations of Englishmen during the Sixteenth and Seventeenth Centuries*, ed. W. C. Hazlitt (London, 1868), p. 68.

mean to suggest therefore that Elizabethan poetry needed the cultivation of beautiful manners in high places to come of age; but I do wish to propose that the *concurrence* of the court's esteem for artistic behavior and the rise of poetic activity in late Tudor England could not but enhance the value of such activity as well as encourage it. And, while my argument does not pretend to explain finally the causes for the remarkable literary efflorescence in England at the end of the sixteenth century, it should serve to modify a widely held view of why it occurred. According to this view the poetic achievements of Elizabethan England were an immediate legacy of Renaissance Humanism, more specifically that they were the fruit of the rhetorical training promoted by humanist educators in the Tudor grammar schools. This belief can be found either asserted or implied in many recent studies of Elizabethan rhetoric and schooling. Here, for example, is how one student of the rhetorical tradition in Tudor England expresses it:

> Of course, nothing can "explain" the flourishing of the arts in any age, but the credit for one of the richest abilities of Renaissance literature, its mastery of the expressive resources of language, must be given directly to the humanist school-system and to the masters who energetically enforced it. . . . For the schools exerted a lasting impression on the writers who attended them— Marlowe at Canterbury, Spenser at Merchant Taylor's (under Mulcaster), Sidney and Fulke Greville at Shrewsbury, Shakespeare almost certainly at Stratford Grammar School. . . . Here they all achieved a "solid grounding" in the most ancient and powerful literary discipline, and within the framework of rhetoric they were free to develop. We owe more to the Elizabethan schoolmaster than we know.[4]

[4] Brian Vickers, *Classical Rhetoric and English Poetry* (London, 1970), pp. 53-54. In his vast study of Tudor grammar-school training, *William Shakespere's Small Latine and Less Greeke*, 2 vols. (Urbana, Ill., 1944), T. W. Baldwin implies that such schooling, "the only formal literary training provided by society in Shake-

Needless to say, the proposal that good schooling was re-
sponsible for the flourishing of poetry is particularly dear
to educators. But the argument is compelling for other
reasons. When one considers the pedagogical devices by
means of which the Renaissance student learned to com-
municate effectively—speaking and writing exercises; a
thorough training in the ornamental processes of rhetoric;
paraphrasing, translating, and imitating classical literature,
including, of course, the ancient poets—it is most tempting
to attribute the growth of poetic expression in the Renais-
sance to humanist education. Clearly literature, in its broad-
est sense, profited greatly from the rhetorical orientation
humanists gave to the curriculum. After reading T. W.
Baldwin's enormous study of grammar-school training in
Shakespeare's day or D. L. Clark's similar but more engag-
ing account of Milton's education, there is no denying that
this schooling was responsible for shaping the communica-
tive skills and developing the verbal energies so evident in
the period.[5] Poetry, too, could only gain in status by being
included as a field of study in the curriculum. But the ap-
preciation and imitation of classical poets encouraged in the
Renaissance grammar school, let alone the rhetorical disci-
pline the schools provided, were not intended as training in
poetic diction. Orators and articulate citizens, *not* poets,

---

speare's day," directly stimulated the production of Elizabethan
poetry. Similarly, in her pioneering study of Tudor rhetoric Sister
Miriam Joseph writes that the Renaissance schoolmasters "cultivated
the ground from which flowered the great vernacular literatures.
Ariosto, Ronsard, and Shakespeare learned through training in Latin
to write superbly in their own tongues." *Shakespeare's Use of the
Arts of Language* (New York. 1947), p. 8. For some sage reserva-
tions about Sister Miriam Joseph's study and its implicit attempt to
make simple "causal connections between teaching procedures and
outcomes," see I. A. Richards, "The Places and the Figures," in
Speculative Instruments (London, 1955), pp. 156-169, also reprinted
in *Elizabethan Poetry, Modern Essays in Criticism*, ed. Paul Alpers
(New York, 1967), pp. 78-89.

[5] T. W. Baldwin's study is cited above; D. L. Clark, *John Milton
at St. Paul's School* (New York, 1948).

were expected to benefit from these literary exercises and the curriculum in general. One cannot disregard the fact that the pursuit of eloquence was encouraged by humanist educators for purposeful and political rather than playful ends. These teachers wanted their students to speak well so that they could eventually stand in front of other men and make a case for a particular action. It is not unfair to say that they valued social and political uses of literature more than esthetic ones. Their dream was to make all learning, not just literature, politically effective. They failed, however, largely because their aspirations were incompatible with the exigencies of Tudor despotism.

In fact, one reason why modern historians have not taken a favorable view of the court's role in the cultural progress of the sixteenth century is its adverse effect on humanist ideals. One can first note in Italy, where Renaissance humanism originally took root, how the rise of despotic institutions in the *cinquecento* led to the decline of these ideals. Usually, this cultural change is not only observed but lamented. For example, in his authoritative study of the pedagogical theories bequeathed to Europe by *quattrocento* Italian humanists, Eugenio Garin explains how the civic aspirations embodied in their educational program had to be compromised, even abandoned, with the rise of Italian principalities and the progressive dominance of European monarchies. "L'ideale universalmente umano degli *studia humanitatis*," he writes

che intendevano formare l'uomo concreto, entrava in crisi anche in un'altra direzione. Affermatosi negli Stati-città italiani con l'intento preciso di formare il libero cittadino di libera repubblica, ossia di educare tutti alla vita civile, dinanzi all trasformazione politica delle Signorie, al definirsi dei Principati, all'affacciarsi delle monarchie, venne adattandosi variamente alla situazione. In realtà all' azione politica, e cioè a quella pienezza di "vita civile" a cui aveva guardato un Palmieri, ben pochi erano destinati, e anch' essi a diverso livello: i reggitori veri e propri,

ossia i principi, e i loro ministri e collaboratori, e in genere
uomini del loro mondo, ossia i "cortegiani." L'ideale del
cittadino di repubblica, di città come Firenze, lascia il
posto al principe e al cortegiano; e mentre i libri sull'
educazione del principe nella loro parte tecnica sono
opere di scienza politica, a cui corrisponderanno, sul piano
più strettamente professionale, le opere sul segretario o
sul cancelliere, sul piano del costume di un intero gruppo
sociale in qualche modo partecipe del potere troviamo
scritti come *Il Cortegiano* del conte Baldassar Castiglione,
che ebbe del resto una grande fortuna europea. Il cortegi-
ano non è più libero cittadino di libera repubblica, che è
sempre anche sovrano; è uomo di corte, al servizio del
sovrano, vicino al principe e suo collaboratore. Qui, a
volte, sembrano permanere le forme dell' educazione
umanistica; ma sono sopratutto le forme; la *cortegiania*,
la *gentilezza*, l'abilità, la cultura che serve, che diventa
strumento raffinato di una precisa tecnica. La cultura non
è formativa di una personalità integralmente libera . . . è
solo formale, forma esteriore che definisce precisi rap-
porti.[6]

[6] The universally human ideal of the *studia humanitatis*, which
aimed to shape the active civic man, also underwent a crisis in an-
other way. Having affirmed itself in the city-states of Italy with the
specific intent of forming a free citizen of a free republic, that is of
educating all men to participate in civic life, this ideal adapted itself
in various ways when faced with the political transformations of the
signories, the establishment of principates, and the emergence of mon-
archies. In fact, very few were destined to partake in political action,
that fullness of "civic life" that a Palmieri had envisioned, and even
those few—the actual governors, that is to say the princes, and their
ministers and collaborators and, in general, men of their world,
namely "courtiers"—were politically active on a different level. The
ideal of the republican citizen, of a city like Florence, gives way to
that of the prince and the courtier. While books on the prince's
education are, in their technical aspects, works of political science to
which will correspond, on a narrower professional level, treatises on
the secretary and the councillor, at the level of manners of a whole
social group at the center of power we find texts such as Count Bal-
dassare Castiglione's *Cortegiano*, a book that enjoyed, by the way, a

The time lag occurring before the cultural program of Italian humanism was assimilated in France and England and other countries beyond the Alps where monarchic rule was already established meant that humanist values had to submit to rival courtly ideals more immediately than they may have had to in Italy.[7] But the shift from a humanist to a courtly ideal of the cultured man, which Garin broadly describes, was not only an Italian but a European phenomenon in the sixteenth century. Garin's account of the court's ascendance as a center of cultural authority displays, however, a typically republican bias. For him the social and political dominance of courtly institutions represents a setback for cultural progress since it brings with it the loss of political freedom and the hollowing of a dignified vision of man. One could not surmise from his account that the rise of Renaissance despotism could have induced any worthy achievements. His profound sympathy for humanist ideology makes it almost impossible for him to attribute anything positive to the forces that frustrated its goals. To sug-

---

great success in Europe. The courtier is no longer a free citizen of a free republic, still granted sovereign rights; he is a man of the court, in the service of the sovereign, a man close to the prince and his collaborator. Here, at times, the forms of humanist education seem to survive, but mainly the forms: courtliness, politeness, tactful skill, culture that serves, that becomes the refined instrument of a precise technique. Culture is no longer formative of a wholly free personality . . . it becomes solely formal, an external form used to define specific and precise relations. Eugenio Garin, *L'educazione in Europe 1400-1600* (Bari, 1966), pp. 140-141. [My translation.]

[7] I am aware that the term "humanism" has acquired many meanings and that, as a cultural movement in the Renaissance, humanism took on a variety of shapes. When I use the term or refer to "humanist values" I have in mind primarily the civic and pedagogical program first advanced in fifteenth-century Italy by spokesmen like Salutati, Bruni, Vergerio, Vittorino da Feltre, and Guarino, and later disseminated in Northern Europe and England (with some modifications) by Erasmus, Vives, Colet, Melanchthon, Sturm, and Ascham. It will become clearer that the aspect of this program on which I particularly dwell is its renewal and promotion of the Isocratean-Ciceronian ideal of making learning and eloquences socially and politically effective.

gest, as he could have suggested, that the changes he discerns stimulated the development of the fine arts and, in particular, imaginative literature would contradict his insistence on cultural decline. It would invite the thought that the artistic accomplishments of the age were less the legacy of an admirable pedagogical movement than the consequences of the failure of humanist educators to achieve their social and political goals.[8]

A similar sympathy for the pedagogical ideals of humanism prompts the argument that their practice in Tudor grammar schools led directly to the flourishing of poetry. The argument is insufficient and therefore misleading. In my opinion the humanist aspirations instilled in the schools played a lesser role in stimulating poetic production than the courtly values that, as Garin points out, displaced or denied those aspirations. First of all, in comparison to the

[8] One important reason why the cultural achievements of the Renaissance have been linked to the republican ideology fashioned in the city-states of Florence and Venice is that this century's finest historical scholars of the Renaissance have been partial, for political reasons, to such ideology. The republican bias one can perceive in Eugenio Garin's remarks about the shift from civic to courtly ideals in sixteenth-century Italy (see also his final comments in the Introduction to *L'Educazione Umanistica in Italia. Testi scelti e illustrati*, a cura di Eugenio Garin (Bari, 1949; rept. 1964), pp. 9-10) is particularly manifest in the studies of Hans Baron, especially his important and influential *Crisis of the Early Italian Renaissance: Civic Humanism and Republican Liberty in an Age of Classicism and Tyranny* (Princeton, 1955; rev. ed. 1966). For an interesting account of the relation between Hans Baron's political biography and his view of the Florentine republic's decisive role in shaping Renaissance culture see Renzo Pecchioli, " 'Umanesimo civile' e interpretazione 'civile' dell' Umanesimo," *Studi Storici* 13 (1972), 3-33.

Burckhardt, it should be recalled, had emphasized the role of the "tyrant" courts in stimulating the new social and cultural developments that, in his view, characterized the civilization of the Renaissance. Whether or not it attests Burckhardt's continuing influence, there is now, nonetheless, an upsurge of historical interest in the despotic states of *quattrocento* and *cinquecento* Italy and their contributions to Renaissance culture. Notable among recent American contributions of this kind is Werner L. Gundersheimer's *Ferrara: The Style of a Renaissance Despotism* (Princeton, 1973).

schools, the court tended to be indifferent to Latin and much more hospitable to English; it therefore played a vital role in encouraging the efforts of Tudor writers to make their native tongue more eloquent. But it was not just the court's preference for the vernacular that stimulated the growth of English poetry. I want to propose that the verbal energies and skills activated in the school system would not have been reoriented into more playful, more esthetic modes of discourse, would not in some instances have assumed poetic forms, had it not been for the stylistic pressures exerted by dominant courtly taste. To support this claim it will be necessary to show how different the rhetorical stances encouraged by humanists—basically those of the classical orator—were from the rhetorical stances cultivated at court. The difference can illuminate why the civic ideals of humanism clashed with the values governing the conduct of princely establishments. More significantly for the purpose of this study, the difference reveals why poetic discourse could appeal to courtly taste in ways that oratory could not. In turn, the rhetorical compatibility of poetry and courtliness can indicate how the court, when imposing its values on Tudor society, could stimulate poetic modes of expression even while it stifled the more political ones encouraged in the schools.

It has already been proposed that the submission of humanist ideals to the demands of courtly taste led to the growth of imaginative literature in Elizabethan England. G. K. Hunter makes this argument in the lively introduction to his study of John Lyly.[9] Examining the transition summed up by Garin as it occurred in Tudor England, Hunter describes how literate men schooled in the new humanist methods had to modify their values to comply with those prevailing at Elizabeth's court, where they hoped for preferment. The "myth of the political effectiveness of learning" instilled during their training made them gravitate to the royal center of power, which, they discovered, was

[9] G. K. Hunter, *John Lyly, The Humanist as Courtier* (Cambridge, Mass., 1962), pp. 1-35.

ready to exploit and be entertained by their verbal skills but was hardly dependent on the political use of their eloquence. "Thus," Hunter writes, "the tradition of practical learning and ethical preoccupation which brought the Humanists to the court was met with a requirement that they use their literary gifts and forget their ideals, that they abandon their internationalist, pacific, and misogynist impulses and become the encomiasts of tournaments, of hunting, and of amorous dalliance. Petrarch could complain 'Where do we read that Cicero or Scipio jousted?' but this reaction was hardly open to the Tudor court entertainer." Hunter proposes that a humanist turned courtier, like John Lyly, virtually made literature out of the frustrations imposed by this predicament. "The literature of the 'eighties and 'nineties," he goes on to say, "is, in fact, largely a product of frustration. . . . As treatises on the (political) fruits of learning give way to defences of poetry, as the scope open to eloquence shrinks from statecraft through polemic to mere entertainment so the 'University Wits' of the period have to contain their sense of divine mission within the bounds of a poor pamphlet. The eventual result of this union of learning and the need for popularity, of moral zeal and profane forms, is the greatest literature our language has known."[10]

The virtue of this interpretation, generalized as it may be, is that, unlike others, it entertains the benefits for imaginative literature stemming from the denial of humanist aspirations. Professor Hunter recognizes that the exigencies of the royal establishment, while depriving men of free political expression and participation, could serve to redirect eloquence into less socially immediate but more esthetic modes of expression. Despite his antipathies toward the values that governed a despotic court like Elizabeth's, unlike many students of Tudor literature, he acknowledges the impact of these values on the growth of artistic expression. He is willing to countenance the disturbing possibility

---

[10] *Ibid.*, p. 31 and p. 34.

that admirable esthetic achievements can be the product of social and political conditions we may consider detestable, that the loss of political freedom, especially the loss of free speech, may be in certain cases a gain for poetic art. Yet aware as Hunter makes us of the court's agency in redirecting verbal energies into more poetic forms, he casts the institution in no better light than Garin. He, too, refuses to see the *virtues* of court style or the more favorable conditions poets enjoyed with its ascendancy. By insisting that the choice to produce imaginative literature results from the frustrations imposed by courtly values, he overlooks the encouragement they extended. This is where my view of the court's role differs from his. Although social and political limitations condition it, the stimulus to write poetry was prompted by the sympathies of the courtly milieu. Rather than having a frustrating effect, the court's values served poets as a source of support and justification for their art. My account seeks to give the court's playful and esthetic inclinations, and its norms of comportment generally, a more positive appraisal than Hunter and others have been willing to grant them. Courtliness deserves this reassessment; what's more, by redeeming some of its virtues, we find it easier to understand why a court like Elizabeth's helped to foster poetic activities.

An awareness that poetry could benefit from the example of proper court style existed among Elizabethans themselves. Its fullest expression is to be found in one of the major critical treatises of the period: Puttenham's *Arte of English Poesie* (1589). The directives prescribed for the poet in this work are drawn, as I will show, from observed norms of courtliness. In fact, Puttenham's correlation of poetic and courtly conduct effectively reveals some of their affinities, which I intend to make clearer. By drawing these affinities on the basis of model comportment he claims to have witnessed, the author attests that the kind of artistic self-fashioning prescribed by Castiglione was cultivated at Elizabeth's court. Puttenham actually maintains that, at the time his treatise was composed, Elizabethan poetry still lacked the artistry and refinement already achieved in court behavior. By showing would-be poets how to develop the resources of their art to attain the sophistication of such behavior, he reveals to us the mutual features poetry shared with proper court style and the gains poets could enjoy as a result of this mutuality.

However, the relationship drawn in the *Arte* between courtliness and poetry—that the courtier's beautiful conduct can serve as an example to the poet as well as authorize his verbal artifices—could not be long sustained, but not just because Elizabethan poets achieved stylistic mastery more quickly than Puttenham anticipated. Ties between poetry and court conduct served to enhance what poets did only as long as that conduct won the admiration of Englishmen; as long as Elizabethans continued to believe in the myth of the perfect courtier, that is, poets could rely on the authority of court manners to justify their art. Puttenham's treatise itself suggests why the myth won such credence: for a time it was effectively cultivated and promoted by Queen Elizabeth and those around her. But by the end of her reign, as I will show in the latter part of my study, Englishmen began to lose their faith in perfect courtliness. So in the 1590s poets found it increasingly necessary to dissociate their art from court conduct, now more often seen to be the corruption rather than the cultivation of beautiful manners. Yet the dissociation was not complete. Puttenham considered the courtier as society's arbiter of style and proposed that the poet could perfect his verbal conduct by imitating proper court manners. But when the faith in exemplary courtliness waned a decade after Puttenham's *Arte* was written, this assumption was reversed. In the absence of any courtly models of comportment, the poet's special attributes (so similar to those of the courtier as he had been idealized) qualify *him* as society's maker of manners, and he emerges as the one who can impart lessons of conduct to the courtier.

In my concluding chapter I examine how this idea—that the courtier must turn to the poet to learn proper courtesy

—is subtly expressed in the Sixth Book of *The Faerie Queene*. Like Puttenham, Spenser assumes that the same principles that constitute beauty in human conduct serve to beautify poetic art. However, Spenser's conception of courteous conduct as a poetic phenomenon will serve to support his claim that the poet is uniquely endowed to understand as well as to teach courtesy. While his image of the poet as the nation's maker of manners has a history going back to antiquity, my larger argument will show that it has another, more specific history in Elizabethan culture. For that image could not be projected until the Elizabethan poet felt secure enough about his vocation to claim that he was more qualified to legislate beautiful manners than the courtier, the individual who, for a time, in England, had been entrusted to fulfill that role.

Chapter I
Sixteenth-century courtiers cultivated rhetorical stances that differed from the rhetorical ideals pursued by the humanists. By considering the differences between courtly and humanist rhetoric we can begin to see why poets gained from the ascendance of courtly values and also why the court played a more decisive role in stimulating poetry than did the Renaissance school. Perhaps the most effective way of appreciating these differences is to compare two texts that embody, respectively, courtly and humanist conceptions of the civilized man: Castiglione's *Book of the Courtier* and Cicero's *De oratore*. The grounds for using Castiglione's book to define the sixteenth-century ideal of court conduct are obvious enough. Its status as *the* mirror of Renaissance courtliness is already evident in the number of European printings it received—over eighty editions of *The Courtier* in Italian and in various translations were published between 1528 and 1619.[1] But why choose Cicero's *De oratore* to represent the humanist ideal of the civilized man?

The international movement we call Renaissance humanism expressed its social, intellectual, and moral values in eclectic ways. The various and often conflicting modern in-

---

[1] The dates of the first translations of the *Cortegiano* in Spanish (1534), French (1537), English (1561), and German (1566) offer one index of its expanding European influence. While originally meant to serve a commemorative as well as a prescriptive function, the work was primarily read as a handbook of manners outside Italy. For more about the influence and status of the *Cortegiano* as an art of conduct in Europe, see, among other studies: Margherita Moreale, *Castiglione y Boscan: El Ideal Cortesano en el Renascimento Espanol* (Madrid, 1959); Reinhard Klesczewski, *Die französischen Übersetzungen des Cortegiano von Baldassare Castiglione* (Heidelberg, 1966); Walter Schrinner, *Castiglione und die englische Renaissance* (Berlin, 1939). H. R. Trevor-Roper mentions in passing that "at least sixty editions and translations" of *The Courtier* appeared between 1528 and 1619. (See *Crisis in Europe 1560-1660*, ed. Trevor Aston (London, 1965), p. 80.) By my count, based on references to editions in studies mentioning the text, and on catalogue entries, his estimate is low.

terpretations of humanism attest to its protean character.[2] Nevertheless, since Paul Kristeller pointed out that humanism consisted of a cultural and educational program chiefly concerned with rhetoric, philology, and scholarship, that it was, as he puts it, "a characteristic phase in what may be called the rhetorical tradition in Western culture," it has been generally recognized that rhetoric played a central role in humanist culture and that the pursuit of eloquence united its many aspirations.[3] Early Italian humanists did not

[2] For a concise review of the various modern interpretations of Renaissance Humanism see Donald Weinstein, "In Whose Image and Likeness? Interpretations of Renaissance Humanism," *JHI* 33 (1972), 165-176.

[3] P. O. Kristeller's influential definition of humanism as a phase of the rhetorical tradition that began with the Greek Sophists is to be found in his *Renaissance Thought, The Classic, Scholastic, and Humanist Strains* (New York, 1961), Ch. i. In Ch. v of the book, "Humanism and Scholasticism in the Renaissance," Kristeller further establishes that humanism was not a philosophical movement but rather an educational enterprise chiefly preoccupied with rhetoric, philology and scholarship. Most of the subsequent studies on the rhetorical orientation of humanism have been indebted to Kristeller's observations. Hanna Gray provides the most succinct account of this rhetorical orientation in "Renaissance Humanism: The Pursuit of Eloquence," *JHI* 24 (1963), 497-514. "The bond which united humanists," she writes, "no matter how far separated in outlook or in time, was a conception of eloquence and its uses. Through it, they shared a common intellectual method and a broad agreement on the value of that method. Classical rhetoric—or classical rhetoric as interpreted and adapted in the Renaissance—constituted the main source for both. It provided the humanists with a body of precepts for the effective communication of ideas and, equally important, with a set of principles which asserted the central role of rhetorical skill and achievement in human affairs" (p. 498). For a useful account of the humanists' concern, as rhetoricians, with the competing claims of eloquence and wisdom, and their attempt to reconcile them, see Jerrold Seigel, *Rhetoric and Philosophy in Renaissance Humanism: The Union of Eloquence and Wisdom, Petrarch to Valla* (Princeton, 1968). The central role of rhetoric in humanist culture is explored in Michael Baxandall, *Giotto and the Orators* (Oxford, 1971), esp. Ch. i, "Humanists' Opinions and Humanist Points of View." See also Nancy Struever, *The Language of History in the*

call themselves by that name but rather identified themselves as orators. Their occupations often consisted of teaching or practicing rhetoric and, generally, they wanted to be known as men of eloquence. Ever since Petrarch had rediscovered the scope and status of classical rhetoric, the humanists sought to give their calling the dignity and importance oratory had received in ancient Rome. Their program of education in the classics, the *studia humanitatis*, which would give them their subsequent appellation, aimed to make men live well and speak well. Actually, from their point of view, living well was inseparable from mastering the art of *bene dicendi*. They wanted rhetoric to become the basic cultural discipline it had been in Cicero's time and they argued that the possession of eloquence was more important than the acquisition of abstract knowledge, even though they sought, following Cicero's example, to combine eloquence and wisdom. While no humanist could ultimately become an orator, as Cicero had been one, the latter's oratorical practice as well as his theoretical standards became the pattern to emulate. "The humanists," writes Hanna Gray, who provides the finest recent summary of the pursuit of eloquence that identifies them,

> followed the Ciceronian tradition also in their portrait of the orator as hero. The true orator, they maintained, should combine wide learning, extensive experience— and, according to most humanists, good character—with persuasive capacity. His role was to instruct, to delight and to move men toward worthwhile goals. His eloquence would represent a unity of content, structure, and form, without ever losing sight of the sovereignty of substance or of the didactic aims which were to be realized . . . through the cooperation of argument and style. Without his eloquence, truth would lie mute, knowledge would never serve the reality of human affairs or speak to the needs of worldly existence. The other arts would

Renaissance: Rhetoric and Historical Consciousness in Florentine Humanism (Princeton, 1970).

be lost, society ill-organized; justice might not triumph nor evil be vanquished. The humanists' *uomo universale*, if such there was, is to be found in their picture of the ideal orator, master of many arts and governor of his fellowmen, through the force of his eloquence forging a link between the intellectual and practical spheres of human experience.[4]

Of the classical texts that embodied this ideal, two of the basic ones for Renaissance humanists were Cicero's *De oratore* and Quintilian's *Institutio Oratoria*. Though both works had been known in the Middle Ages, their influence became much more pronounced after complete texts were rediscovered in the early fifteenth century (Quintilian's full text was found in 1416, Cicero's in 1421 along with the *Brutus* and *Orator*). That *De oratore* was one of the very first books printed in Italy (Subiaco, 1466) is an indication of the cultural importance it acquired among fifteenth-century humanists. Reprinted continually thereafter, by itself or together with Cicero's other treatises on rhetoric, it became one of the best known books in Renaissance Europe. It was especially as a school and university text that it exerted enormous influence in the sixteenth century. Surviving academic curricula show that it was assigned for reading and commentary in the final grades of Renaissance schools and even more frequently recommended for study at the college level, serving, it would seem, as the capstone of all previous rhetorical training.[5] Quintilian's *Institutio* played

[4] Hanna Gray, "Renaissance Humanism: The Pursuit of Eloquence," p. 504.

[5] There exists a large number of studies on Cicero's enormous influence in the fifteenth and sixteenth centuries as well as on the nature of Renaissance ciceronianism. Few of them devote much attention to the fortunes of *De oratore* specifically, though they frequently acknowledge its importance among humanists. See, for example, Remigio Sabbadini, *Storia del Ciceronianismo* (Torino, 1885); Izora Scott, *Controversies over the Imitation of Cicero* (New York, 1910), esp. pp. 112-124; Giuseppe Toffanin, *Storia dell'umanesimo* (Bologna, 1965), esp. Ch. II, pp. 100-116. A. B. Modersohn's survey, "Cicero im Englischen Geistleben des 16. Jahrunderts," *Archiv für das Studium*

an equally important role in shaping the humanist image of the orator, but it was especially influential for its educational theory regarding the early training of orators.[6] Actually

---

der neueren Sprachen und der Literaturen 80 (1926), 33-51 and 219-245, shows that of all Cicero's rhetorical works, *De oratore* is the most frequently cited in Tudor England.

We still lack a study of the humanist commentaries on *De oratore*. In one of the standard sixteenth-century collections of commentaries on Cicero's rhetorical works, *In Omnes De Arte Rhetorica M. Tul. Ciceronis Libros Doctissimorum Vivorum Commentaria . . .*, originally published in Basel in 1541, the first and by far the longest is the commentary on *De oratore* by Strebaeus Remensis. The latter's praise of *De oratore* in his preface to Francis I already serves to explain the priority it is given: "Rhetorica Ciceronis ad Quintum fratrem, citra omnem controversiam superant omnia quae de arte dicendi & a Graecis, & a Latinis memoriae sunt prodita. . . . Nusquam tam magnifice honore vestitur orator, nusquam ita graviter & ornate demonstratur oratoria facultas. . . . Sic iudico, omnes omnium rhetorum scriptas observationes in unum coactas, cum hoc uno opere neque gravitate, neque varietate, neque elegantia neque alia laude comparari posse." ["Disputes aside, Cicero's rhetoric to his brother Quintus surpasses everything recorded on the subject of eloquence by both Greeks and Latins. Nowhere is the orator clad in such splendid dignity, nowhere is oratory described so gravely and ornately. . . . I maintain that the writings of all the other teachers of oratory united together cannot stand comparison with this one work either in terms of gravity, or variety, or elegance, or any other merit."—My translation]

[6] For a survey of Quintilian's influence on humanist pedagogy see August Messer, "Quintilian als Didaktiker und sein Einfluss auf die didaktisch-pädagogische Theorie des Humanismus," *Neue Jahrbücher für Philologie und Pädagogik* 67 (1897), 161-204, 273-292, 321-336, 361-387, 409-423, 457-473.

It must be said that, while Italian humanists drew their ideals of eloquence from both Cicero and Quintilian, they distinguished the theories of the two Roman authors. By the later *quattrocento* Cicero and Quintilian can be seen to exert rival influences as rhetoricians. In his recent study, *Lorenzo Valla, Umanesimo e Teologia* (Firenze, 1972), Salvatore Camporeale demonstrates the distinct influence of Quintilian's *Institutio* on Valla's philological humanism, and he suggests that Valla's preference for Quintilian over Cicero, which provoked significant controversy among his fellow humanists, lies at the root of the anti-ciceronianism later expressed by Poliziano and Erasmus.

much of the humanist theory devoted to shaping eloquent men emphasized their early training instead of portraying the adult orator as he should function in the world. One reason humanists stressed the pedagogical uses of classical rhetoric—the training it provided in sheer verbal technique and virtuosity—rather than its political and judicial uses was that the institutional functions oratory had enjoyed in ancient courts of law and public assemblies became much more limited in the Renaissance, even in the city-states of Italy. Nonetheless, the ideal aim of the rhetorical education advocated by humanists remained utilitarian and civic: to make men capable of communicating political and ethical truths so persuasively that they would thereby reform and civilize society. The importance and singularity of Cicero's *De oratore* lay in offering an authoritative model of the orator performing such a role. Its secular orientation notwithstanding, the ideal of the eloquent man fashioned in Cicero's book came close to representing the exemplary citizen that humanist education sought to produce.

Cicero's *De oratore* lends itself particularly well to a comparison with Castiglione's *Courtier* because the latter work also devotes itself to the portrayal of an adult individual acting in society. Pointing out similarities between the two works confirms, incidentally, what Castiglione was the first to acknowledge: his use of Cicero's book as one of the principal models for his own. And given the authority and prominence of *De oratore* in the Renaissance, when *The Courtier* appeared in 1528 it could only be enhanced by its recognizable imitation of the Latin work. Thomas Hoby pointed out the resemblances between the two works when his English translation of Castiglione appeared in 1561:

> Were it not that the ancientnes of time, the degree of a Consul, and the eloquence of Latin stile in these our dayes beare a great stroke, I know not whither in the invention and disposition of the matter, as Castilio hath followed Cicero, and applyed to his purpose sundrie examples and pithie sentences out of him, so he may in feat conveyance

and like trade of wryting, be compared to him: But wel
I wot, for renowme among the Italians, he is not inferi-
our to him. Cicero an excellent Oratour, in three books
of an Oratour unto his brother, fashioneth such a one as
never was, nor yet is like to be: Castilio an excellent
Courtier, in three bookes of a Courtier unto his deare
friend, fashioneth such a one as is hard to find and per-
haps unpossible. Cicero bringeth in to dispute of an Ora-
tour, Crassus, Antonius, Cotta, Sulpitius, Catullus and Ce-
sar his brother, the noblest and chiefest Oratours in those
daies. Castilio, to reason of a Courtier, the Lord Octavian
Fregoso, Sir Frideric his brother, the Lord Julian de
Medecis, the Lord Cesar Ganzaga, the L. Frances Co-
maria Della Rovere, Count Lewis of Canossa, the Lord
Gaspar Pallavisin, Bembo, Bibiena and other most excel-
lent Courtiers, and of the noblest families in these daies
in Italie. . . . Both Cicero and Castilio professe, they fol-
ow not any certaine appointed order of precepts or rules,
as is used in the instruction of youth, but call to rehearsall,
matters debated in their times too and fro in the dispu-
tation of most eloquent men and excellent wittes in every
worthy qualitie, the one company in the olde time as-
sembled in Tusculane, and the other of late yeares in the
new Pallace of Urbin. . . .[7]

A desire for symmetry makes Hoby overlook that *The
Courtier* has four rather than three books, but he does
neatly bring out the broader parallels that have continued
to be recognized in the two works. However, it is not their
similarities but their differences that I wish to stress in the
following comparison. By seeing these differences, especial-
ly between the rhetorical stances the two institutes rec-
ommend, we can more fully understand why the oratori-
cal ideal championed by civic humanists proved incom-
patible with ascending courtly taste. On the other hand, the
contrast already suggests why less utilitarian, more playful

[7] *The Book of the Courtyer*, trans. Sir Thomas Hoby (London,
1561; rept. London: Everyman's Library, 1959), p. 3.

discourse like poetry would be agreeable to courtly norms of conduct. Indeed, the contrast allows us to infer what, eventually, I intend to show explicitly: that the stylistic features of model courtliness resemble poetry's and, hence, their cultivation was bound to encourage and authorize their equivalents in verbal art.

Hoby correctly observed the similarity in settings for the conversations of *De oratore* and *The Courtier*. Both Cicero's Tusculan villa and Castiglione's drawing room are places of leisure and respite, where men find occasion to make ideal projections of themselves. Yet it is soon evident that the two works differ in the relation of their respective settings to the world inhabited by the model individual fashioned in them. Cicero's orator operates in the law court, the senate, the forum, any place of public assembly, not in a suburban villa. His is not a world of relaxed seclusion or of harmonious relations, but one of confrontation, struggle, and strife. Frequently, Cicero's speakers resort to martial imagery to describe the orator's verbal occupation. After preparatory training, "Oratory," says Crassus, "must be conducted out of this sheltered training-ground at home, right into action, into the dust and uproar, into the camp and the fighting-line of public debate."[8] *In foro tamque in acie*. Such military imagery reflects a basic assumption held by the speakers: that oratory is a sublimated form of warfare. Moreover, the villa-garden, where the conversations take place, offers conviviality and privacy. In his occupation, however, the orator becomes totally public yet isolated unless, by the force of eloquence, he wins men's consent and allegiance. True, at several moments in Cicero's dialogue the speakers do represent themselves as antagonists in the forum or the law court, but for the most part their reputa-

---

[8] Cicero, *De oratore*, I. 157. See also I. 32. And later, for instance, Antonius tells the would-be orator that "a panoplied antagonist confronts you who must be smitten as well as countered" (II. 72). Translations of Cicero's texts are taken from the Loeb Classical Library edition of *De oratore*, trans. E. W. Sutton and H. Rackham (Cambridge, Mass., 1967), 2 vols.

tion and skills are not as severely tried in the intimate company gathered at the villa as in the public arena, where verbal triumph becomes the chief test of ability. Most important, the orator in the world can never assume an audience of peers; he exposes himself to all of society. The all-inclusive audience he is called to address requires that he accommodate his conduct, his intellectual range, his style in general to that audience's average capacities.

In contrast, the setting of the conversations in Castiglione's book is much more part of the world usually inhabited by the courtier. The Urbino parlor game devoted to the creation of an ideal courtier is meant to illustrate the kind of profitable recreation such a courtier should pursue. A correspondence between the social setting of the discussions and that of their subject is emphasized by the deliberate resemblance between the speakers' conduct and the proper manners they advocate. This is, by the way, how the author intended to commemorate the civilized achievement of Urbino: by showing that the behavior of its courtiers in reality could approximate an ideal of courtiership imagined in a game. Although the drawing room is an evening retreat within the palace, a good part of the courtier's activity occurs in such places despite the priority given to his military attributes. Unlike Cicero's orator, the courtier often practices his vocation in the kind of sheltered and exclusive milieu in which he is described. Much as the image he presents to beholders shapes his conduct, the courtier's identity is not determined, like the orator's, by his power to persuade other men. His attributes do grant him the power to please, but his functions are virtually as apolitical as the setting in which he is defined, at least until the last evening when Ottaviano seeks to impose on him a political and ethical role. Whereas the orator has to confront the crowd, the courtier's audience consists of familiar and equal company and he hardly needs venture out from his secure enclave at the top of a hierarchal society. On the contrary, to consolidate his privileged exclusion he deliberately cultivates a style that will distinguish him from the ordinary multitude. The courtier can disregard social inferiors since he can avoid intercourse with them. He does, however, remain subject to his prince, and the proper relation to his one superior determines fundamental aspects of his conduct. Just as he cultivates a style that asserts his difference from social subordinates, so he must study to make that style ingratiating to his ruler.

The orator owes service to the individual or to the case he is defending and, more broadly, to the public good of his state; the courtier owes service to his sovereign and then to his lady, or ladies in general. For, quite unlike the orator, he lives in a milieu remarkable for the prominent role it accords to women. Their influence is demonstrated, again, by the setting as well as the description of *The Courtier*. Men may be the main speakers defining the ideal, but they participate in a game governed by a woman. Emilia Pia's arbitration represents the degree to which court conduct is conditioned by female inclinations. Despite objections from misogynists in the group, the participants are quite committed to the idea that the refined civilization they pursue is prompted and enhanced by the presence of women. At the start of the third book, which actually devotes itself to fashioning the female counterpart of the ideal courtier, Gonzaga sums up the civilizing influence of women when he says, "Just as no court, however great, can have adornment or splendor or gaiety in it without ladies, neither can any Courtier be graceful or pleasing or brave, or do any gallant deed of chivalry, unless he is moved by the society and by the love and charm of ladies" (III. 3, pp. 204-205).[9] Since the possibility that women could assume an oratorical role is inconceivable in Cicero's work, it disregards their existence. The irrelevance of women to the orator's activity as op-

[9] Here and henceforth I cite from Baldesar Castiglione, *The Book of the Courtier*, trans. Charles Singleton (Garden City, N.Y., 1959). Citations will be followed by page references to this text, preceded by a reference to book and section for the reader who may wish to consult the Italian text in a standard edition such as *Il Libro del Cortegiano*, ed. Bruno Maier (Torino, 1962), or *Il Cortegiano*, ed. Vittorio Cian (Firenze, 1929³).

posed to their decisive influence on the courtier's can illumi-
nate subtle differences between attributes the two appear to
have in common. Consider, for example, the liberal and
broad education both individuals are asked to acquire.

"No man can be an orator complete in all points of merit,"
claims Cicero at the beginning of his work, "who has not at-
tained a knowledge of all important subjects and arts. For
it is from knowledge that oratory must derive its beauty
and fullness, and unless there is such knowledge, well-
grasped and comprehended by the speaker, there must be
something empty and childish in the utterance" (I. 20). The
author echoes here Crassus' own demand throughout the
dialogue that the orator be generally cultured and able to
command vast areas of knowledge. Antonius will challenge
the claims that the orator must master all of philosophy as
well as private and public law, and, in general, the range of
the orator's learning becomes a dominant issue of debate in
the work. But some consensus is reached. The orator's nec-
essary training in the liberal arts is an unchallenged requi-
site, and it is partly for the sake of argument that Antonius
denies in the first book the necessity of wide-ranging cul-
ture, for in the second he concedes "that all things relating
to the intercourse of fellow citizens and the ways of man-
kind . . . must be mastered by the orator" (II. 68). The
orator remains a non-specialist because of the range of issues,
topics, and situations he must confront. Cicero's speakers
recognize that without broad training the orator will fail to
convince the variety of professionals and publics he must be
ready to address. They acknowledge realistically that his
breadth must often make up for his depth of knowledge in
certain fields. But this does not mean that he can afford to
be a dilettante. Nor does general culture remain a source of
private satisfaction; it is to be used for the public good. The
orator is not admired for his wide-ranging knowledge as
such but for the way his eloquence can make that knowl-
edge work on men's wills. Ultimately, the limits and oc-
casional superficiality of his knowledge are outweighed by

his ability to make it prompt men to action in a way that the learned but uneloquent specialist cannot do.

"I would have him more than passably learned in letters, at least in those studies which we call the humanities" (I. 44, p. 70). So Ludovico introduces his discussion of the courtier's cultural requisites. Though he is challenged when he proposes that the courtier should also acquire skills in arts not traditionally liberal, the scope of education does not become the central issue of debate it was in *De oratore*. Ludovico will virtually disregard the moral and intellectual attributes acquired in the broad training he recommends to dwell primarily on its esthetic dimensions. Appreciation as well as practice of literary prose and verse, music, drawing, and painting will most benefit the courtier. These pursuits are justified on the grounds that they will offer him personal solace and enhance his capacity to please those around him, especially the ladies. He is encouraged, moreover, to cultivate the fine arts in order to gather insights about beautiful effects, which he can then apply to the process of his own shaping. Aside from being pleasing for its own sake or as an endowment impressive to behold, the possession of culture and knowledge is not given any larger purpose in the first three books of *The Courtier*. Learning and education seem above all to serve an ornamental function. Like the orator, the courtier may be a non-specialist trained in the liberal arts, but while extensive knowledge serves the former to communicate with all members and professions in his society, it just allows the latter to be a dilettante who uses his versatile gifts to entertain an exclusive and often largely feminine audience.

The possibilities offered the courtier to engage in philosophical discourse and intellectual issues generally are much more curtailed than the orator's. Already in Cicero's work, despite the insistence on philosophical studies, there is a bias against the merely intellectual, ineloquent and therefore socially ineffective discourse of the philosophers. When Antonius expresses this bias, he objects less to the orator's training in philosophy than to the possible outcome: its abstruse and esoteric jargon might color his orations and make them incomprehensible to the untutored general public. This anti-philosophical bias does not mean that the orator must exclude moral issues from his speeches. On the contrary, because moral issues are acknowledged as a common feature of oratory, the orator must communicate them engagingly and intelligibly. The courtier is also expected to acquire some grounding in moral philosophy, but he usually addresses an audience hostile to abstract speculation, professional jargon, even moral disputation. Again, it is among the women in his company that such biases are particularly notable. To accommodate himself to this sort of anti-intellectualism, the courtier has to restrain his philosophical inclinations, if not suppress them altogether. The courtly milieu not only finds the abstruse and austere aspects of philosophy unbecoming, occasions to pursue moral and intellectual subjects are further restricted by the courtly intolerance of unrelieved seriousness. Eloquent and engaging as the orator might make his ethical concerns, the earnestness with which he is asked to express them would not be abided by the audience the courtier usually entertains.

It does not follow, however, that matters of serious import are inevitably made frivolous in the fulfillment of courtly elegance.[10] One of the foremost characteristics of

[10] At least since De Sanctis there exists a critical tradition fond of condemning the playful inclinations of Castiglione's courtiers as well as their artificiality. For an example of such polemicizing against courtly play see Giuseppe Prezzolini's introduction to Baldassar Castiglione and Giovanni della Casa, *Opere* (Milano-Roma, 1937). In a similar vein Giuseppe Toffanin proposes that Castiglione's serious humanist impulses were frustrated and trivialized by the concessions he had to make to frivolous court values. While arguing that in the work a "sapienza umanistica" was impoverished by submitting to courtly ideology, Toffanin quite overlooks that the collocation of the playful and the serious, the ability to shift from the vicissitudes of love to the lofty concerns of model conduct, are precisely what should characterize the behavior of the perfect courtier. See his *Il Cortegiano nella Trattatistica del Rinascimento* (Napoli, 1960), esp. pp. 50-51. To redress this bias against courtly play and orna-

the courtier is a flexible capacity to embody opposites, the difficult moderation that Castiglione calls *mediocrità*. A governing principle in his book, and one that embodies *mediocrità*, is the belief that gravity is made more appealing when it is tempered with levity. The most evident enactment of this principle is the ability of the participants to fashion a human ideal while playing a parlor game. Their willingness to entertain lofty subjects while at play, their capacity for *serio ludere*, serves to exemplify the balance between gravity and facetiousness desired in the perfect courtier. The speakers call upon him to display such flexibility in every aspect of his behavior. Predominant traits determined by age, office, conviction, or state of mind should be balanced by their opposites. *Mediocrità* demands that older men temper their sobriety with light-heartedness, that younger ones balance their boisterous inclinations with sober calm. Similarly, vitality and caution, modesty and pride, fervor and detachment, exhibitionism and reticence must coexist in the graceful personality. So the possession of *sprezzatura*—the ability to disguise artful effort so that it seems natural or to make the difficult appear easy—shown to lend the courtier so much grace also consists of reconciling opposites. *Mediocrità* should also define the ideological outlook of the courtier. Again, the kind of ideological moderation desired can best be observed in the concessions made by Ludovico Canossa in the course of debates he provokes as main speaker in the first book. Whether the issue of controversy be nobility, the proper use of the vernacular, or the debate over arms and letters, Canossa exemplifies the tempered style by eventually accommodating his opinions to opposing opinions; or, at least he is willing to concede the validity of contrary

---

ment, J. A. Mazzeo has argued that, far from being frivolous or trivial, the attention Castiglione's courtiers give to "gesture, manner, games, jokes, and anecdotes" is consistent with the lofty conception of "the self as a work of art," which informs so much of the book. Mazzeo's chapter "Castiglione's *Courtier*: The Self as a Work of Art," in *Renaissance and Revolution* (New York, 1965) remains one of the best general discussions of the work.

views. The claims of politeness and deference restrain the speakers from pleading stubbornly for a particular outlook. Besides, too doctrinaire or reductive a point of view is usually tempered by the mocking qualifications it provokes. In their style and in their temperament the courtiers at Urbino display a marked intolerance and distrust of absolutes or even settled convictions.[11]

Such elasticity in tone, demeanor, and point of view further distinguishes the courtier from the orator. Most of the time the latter's bearing and style display *gravitas* and *auctoritas*. Without forfeiting his dignity he must also, of course, be able to shape himself to the demands of a variety of situations. Cicero's speakers recognize that not only for the different sorts of oratory (i.e., forensic, deliberative, epideictic) but in the practice of one sort, the orator must be ready to display different, often opposing, methods, emotions, and convictions, depending on the occasion. This calls for a theatrical talent similar to the flexibility exhibited by the courtier in the various roles he has to play. The orator, however, is called upon to adapt his style or his *ethos* to the many verbal engagements confronting him. He can hardly be urged, like the courtier, to embody opposing aspects of them simultaneously, for this would defy the partisanship, the earnestness with which he champions or deplores a cause. He seeks, above all, to win both his argument and the consent of his audience, while the courtier, in his detachment, primarily wants to please. The tenacity and aggressiveness required in oratory leave little room for the politeness that requires the courtier to compromise. Not that the courtier lacks aggressive instincts or that competitiveness plays no part in his conduct. On the contrary, it can be said that competition for favor, especially the winning of the prince's favor, motivates much of the courtier's self-display. "Let him," says Ludovico of the model courtier, "put every

[11] For a discussion of the constant play between abstract ideas and lived experience that characterizes Castiglione's dialogue, see Lawrence Lipking, "The Dialectic of *Il Cortegiano*," *PMLA* 81 (1966), 355-362.

effort and diligence into outstripping others in everything a little, so that he may always be recognized as better than the rest" (i. 21, p. 38). But if he seeks to outshine his rivals, the refined manners he must cultivate—a refinement that often consists of sublimating or disguising aggressive instincts—prevent him from competing as overtly as the orator. The more *sprezzatura* and *disinvoltura* the courtier displays to disguise his efforts at outperforming others, the more approbation he wins from both his peers and his sovereign. Again, in the parlor game that takes up their evenings, Castiglione's courtiers demonstrate their competitive urges as well as their ability to subdue them. Clearly one of the functions of game-playing at court is to absorb and disarm the destructive threat of competitive drives. At the same time, however, the controlling circumstances, the rules that govern courtly games, teach the participants to moderate their aggressive impulses in the way deemed desirable when they are not at play.

The orator is allowed to be much more openly combative. It is not surprising, therefore, that moderation is given relatively little attention in *De oratore*. The subject is not disregarded by Cicero's speakers. Antonius advocates moderation when he discusses means of *conciliare*, the ability to ingratiate oneself with the audience so that persuasion can be more easily achieved. "Mildness which wins us good will of our hearers," should be blended, he maintains, with "the fiercest of passions, wherewith we inflame the same people . . . nor is any style better blended than that wherein the harshness of strife is tempered by the personal urbanity of the advocate" (ii. 212). The balance prescribed here resembles the *mediocrità* recommended to the courtier, but the latter's habitual nonchalance hardly calls for the tempering of passionate fervor, which so often dominates oratorical style. Still, Antonius' recommendations at this point in Book ii become increasingly similar to ones proposed in *The Courtier*. After advocating the balancing of fervor and strife with their opposites, he goes on to point out that the usual gravity of the orator will be enhanced if occasionally tempered with wit. This remark prompts the long discussion (II. 217-290) about the nature and function of wit in oratory, much of which Castiglione will borrow for the treatment of the laughable in the second book of his work.

It has always been recognized that Castiglione drew a large portion of his discussion of joke-telling from Cicero's *De oratore*. He even cites the same Roman jokes after transplanting them to a contemporary Italian setting. So obvious is the extent of his borrowing that it obscures how much he adapted his source to accommodate it to courtly imperatives. Yet the differences that can be observed between courtly and oratorical joking, similar though the two appear to be, reveal some of the larger incompatibilities between oratory and courtliness that I wish to indicate. The seriousness and sobriety characterizing Cicero's ideal contribute to a sense that the discussion of jocular tactics, when it comes, is a prolonged digression. Caesar's remark that prefaces his discourse on wit is telling: ". . . of course all this business of laughter-raising is trivial" (II. 219 [Cicero's speaker, C. Julius Caesar Strabo Vopiscus, is not to be confused with the famous general and dictator]). Only by showing how the risible can serve more useful functions than merely prompting pleasure can Caesar reduce its frivolous aspects and reconcile it to the larger serious aims of the orator. When he explains why it becomes an orator to be witty (II. 236), Caesar does not acknowledge the value of gratuitous delight but insists that wit serve persuasion, the chief end of oratory. The orator may rely on humor to attenuate possible hostility toward him or to moderate too austere an appearance, but never in a manner that might jeopardize his *gravitas*. Most frequently he uses humor as a weapon to overcome his opponent. A large number of *facetiae* offered as examples serve to ridicule the opposing "enemy," thereby discrediting his *ethos* and hence his capacity to persuade.[12] As a result,

[12] For some of my remarks on the difference between Cicero's and Castiglione's treatment of joke-telling I draw on Joanna Lipking's study of Renaissance theories of wit, "Traditions of the Facetiae," unpublished Ph.D. dissertation (Columbia University, 1970). When

oratorical joking is rarely pleasant or merely entertaining; it provokes derision rather than delight. And although it "tones down austerity," the fact that it always serves serious and aggressive aims prevents it from being a genuine source of relief.

In *The Courtier* there seems to be nothing digressive about the means and range of joking proper to the courtier, since his bearing and discourse should frequently display a balance between gravity and facetiousness. Wit allows him to achieve this desirable equivocation and is therefore a more integral part of his personality than of the orator's. Moreover, the capacity to raise laughter becomes a necessary talent for a man whose prime function is to please. When the discussion in *The Courtier* turns to the means of inducing laughter, Bibbiena, who acts as Caesar's counterpart, justifies the laughable solely on the grounds that it delights, a motive virtually disregarded in *De oratore*. From the weapon it was to the orator, joking now develops into a recreational activity in itself. Bibbiena makes it clear that pleasure, not disparagement, is the aim of courtly joking by emphasizing much more than does Caesar in Cicero's work the teller's need to be inoffensive and delicate. *Facezie* may expose folly, but their ridicule is aimed more at human foibles in general than the defects of a single individual. Practical jokes, a category of courtly wit not to be found in the Latin source, may provoke laughter at the expense of the deceived, but these jokes are perpetrated for sheer fun, not out of hostility. In his joking, as in debate and controversy, the courtier is asked to attenuate or at least disguise his aggressive instincts in a manner that would prove self-defeating in oratorical combat. Also, since the orator must resort to humor circumspectly—he cannot let it become too

---

discussing Cicero's treatment of jokes in the light of Castiglione's, Lipking stresses that the orator's wit is much more partisan and less amiable than the courtier's. "In essence," she writes, "Cicero sees the joke as an adversary proceeding, a model of the larger oratorical situation in which one man contends with another not only for the best of the argument but for good opinion, authority, face" (p. 279).

distracting—his most effective jokes will be rapid and brief.
While the courtier's quick retort is equally appreciated, the
unhurried, relaxed occasions in which he often provokes
laughter encourage longer anecdotes where the teller's narra-
tive skills contribute as much pleasure as the amusement he
provokes.

It is worth noting that the courtier's verbal wit is an
extension of the *grazia* so desirable in his conduct. Courtly
grace, to the extent that it can be prescribed, is shown to
rely on tactics of dissimulation, which I will discuss more
fully in the next chapter. For instance, *sprezzatura*, one of
the chief sources of such grace, always entails deliberate
subterfuge. This display of seeming nonchalance, and, in
general, the courtier's most esteemed dissimulation are also
usually ironic. For his conduct is deemed most becoming
when he disguises a particular intention, disposition, or abil-
ity by cultivating an appearance of its contrary. The cour-
tier's observers, highly responsive to such indirection, even-
tually see through his graceful guises but enjoy the artifices
that leave them temporarily deceived. Joke-telling offers
further occasion for displaying such grace and is therefore
an integral part of courtliness. For what are the basic verbal
means used in making witticisms? Bibbiena begins his ac-
count of them by suggesting that "quite a nice sort of
pleasantry is that . . . which consists in a certain dissimula-
tion, when one thing is said and another tacitly understood"
(II. 72, p. 169). After examining other ironic devices, like
sarcasm and antithesis, he recommends the witty virtues of
puns, unexpected turns, making disagreeable comments
agreeably, and a number of other ambiguous utterances.
These jocular devices rely, of course, on the same oblique-
ness that contributes so effectively to the courtier's grace.
His activity as a joke-teller thus offers verbal opportunities
to display the kinds of deception so admired in his general
behavior. Originally itemized in *De oratore* (II. 248-264),
these equivocal tactics of wit do not similarly conform to
the bearing or usual verbal style of the orator. The forceful
conviction required of him in making a case can hardly be

accomplished by oblique and ambiguous means. But it is oratory's cardinal rule of clarity that restricts such verbal indirection, whether in witticisms or in any form of address. Just as the orator must vulgarize the intellectual and philosophical contents of his speech in order not to baffle the comprehension of an untutored audience, so if he exploits the figurative resources of language he must do so in a way that aids rather than eludes the common understanding. Admirable as his ornamentation of language may be, any marked departure from normal uses of it might jeopardize his intent to communicate clearly. When Crassus takes up the subject of verbal ornament in Book III he advises the orator to achieve perspicuity "by talking correct Latin, and employing words in customary use that indicate literally the meaning that we desire to be conveyed, and made clear, without ambiguity of language or style, avoiding excessively long periodic structure, not spinning out metaphors drawn from other things. . . ." (III. 49) The necessity for clarity does not inhibit the range of verbal ornament altogether. Crassus goes on to recommend the ornamental virtues of metaphors that, though never literal by definition, often serve by their vividness to make plain what the orator wishes to communicate. Nevertheless, examples of proper metaphorical usage—and this applies to all the ornamental devices Crassus prescribes—are remarkable for their transparency. Whenever he brings up a trope likely to produce ambiguity or veil meaning, he issues a warning against these risks. Crassus' overriding concern for perspicuous language contributes to the sense that the more oblique tropes and devices normally employed in witticisms cannot become regular features of oratory.

Elocutio, the process whereby the orator adorns his speech and delights his auditors, would seem most congenial to the courtly code that so emphasizes the ornamenting of the self. Many of the artifices recommended in the *Cortegiano* for appearing graceful are derived from or resemble the figuration of language and thought that the orator employs to beautify his discourse. Yet the court's distaste for plain and

perspicuous conduct leads to such different esthetic prin-
ciples that the ornamental modes it cherishes are virtually
denied to the orator, expected as he is to be understood by
all. The democratic considerations that underlie oratorical
norms, like clarity, actually serve to illuminate, by contrast,
the social basis of the court's predilection for covert and
deceptive manners. It is not inconsistent that an aristocrat,
convinced of being above or beyond the reach of the com-
mon, should cherish and promote all behavior that refines,
obscures, even defies common usuage. A basic difference
between the orator and the courtier in their use of ornament
is that the former aims to captivate the largest possible
audience while the latter seeks to exclude all but a privileged
few. Castiglione's book repeatedly suggests that the pleasure
derived from the ornamental tactics it recommends will
escape men of plainer and therefore baser taste. Obscurity,
indirection, ambiguity, and deception serve to fulfill such
exclusive ends. The covert methods employed in verbal wit,
for instance, are just part of a repertory of ornamental
tactics that both make the courtier graceful and assert his
social apartness, since the meaning they convey only wins
understanding among the sophisticated. The orator has to
refrain from extensive use of such verbal artifices precisely
because they would isolate him from the broad constituency
he addresses.

The orator, however, need not nor cannot altogether
avoid the deceptive modes so admired in courtly conduct.
Obviously many of the tactics he employs to depart from
normal direct statements—especially "figures of thought,"
such as feigned hesitations, simulated exclamations, irony,
apparent concessions (see III. 202-205)—are fundamentally
deceptive in their nature. More generally, the orator's the-
atricality and his constant effort to appear to best advantage
necessarily call for discrepancies between his being and
seeming. While discussing how to win the sympathies of the
audience, Antonius maintains that a valuable skill is "the
faculty of seeming to be dealing reluctantly and under com-
pulsion with something you are really anxious to prove. . . ."

But the context of this statement reveals how the orator's authenticity is more valued than his occasional deceptions, because just before the statement Antonius considered the orator's *ethos*, the means whereby he establishes his moral integrity and good reputation, so indispensable in gaining the favor of his audience: "Now feelings are won over by a man's merit, achievement, or reputable life, qualifications easier to embellish if only they are real, than to fabricate where non-existent" (II. 182). And shortly after he will argue that whatever indignation or compassion the orator wishes to arouse in his public can only be brought forth if he feels genuinely such emotions in his heart (II. 189). On the whole, the practical recognition that he must resort to deceptive means in some situations seems outweighed by the demands that he hold sincere convictions and be open in the display of his talents. Subterfuge is deemed necessary as an aid to persuasive effect only, and not admired as a source of delightful elegance the way it is in *The Courtier*.

The more one observes the differences between the orator and the courtier, especially in attributes they seem to share, the clearer it becomes that a redistribution of functions constitutes the basic contrast between them. Traditionally the orator must fulfill three functions: to prove (or to instruct), to delight, and to persuade. These three duties are virtually inseparable in that they rely on one another. Persuasion, for instance, will be achieved more effectively if delight accompanies instruction. Nevertheless, as Cicero summed it up in another work, persuasion is the object of highest priority: "Docere debitum est; delectare honorarium; permovere necessarium."[13] In *De oratore* the primacy of persuasion is either asserted (see, for example, II. 178) or, as I have noted,

---

[13] ["It is his (the orator's) duty to instruct; to provide pleasure is a gift; to move is indispensable."] *De optimo genere oratorum*, I, 3. As unsystematic as the speakers in *De oratore* pretend to be, it will be noted that Antonius and Crassus treat the means of fulfilling the orator's three duties in the course of their conversations: Antonius considers *probare* and *movere* in Book II; Crassus takes up *delectare* in Book III.

raised to justify the need of any one of the orator's attri-
butes. Even proof (or instruction) and delight are con-
sidered, primarily, in terms of their effect on the hearer. So
in Book III, when Crassus discusses verbal embellishment,
the means of "delighting," he never dissociates the esthetic
pleasure of ornament from its utility in gaining the audi-
ence's assent. Beautiful norms are constantly determined by
persuasive ones. The cursory consideration of ornament,
taken up rather hurriedly at the end of the discussion, con-
firms the lower priority given esthetic effects in the ranking
of oratorical functions.

Appearing to the best advantage in the opinion of his
beholders motivates the courtier's conduct as much as the
orator's, but for the most part without the latter's persuasive
intent. The prime function of the courtier is to delight,
and a large part of the book devoted to him suggests that
the pleasure produced remains an end in itself. It can be said
that *delectare* assumes the functional priority in courtiership
that *movere* is granted in oratory. Until the final book of
The Courtier delighting is not just a prominent goal, but
nearly the exclusive aim, of the courtier. Only when Ot-
taviano insists on enlarging the role of the ideal courtier do
didactic and persuasive functions take on any real impor-
tance. And the degree to which the courtier, as he has been
defined, can absorb the new functions prescribed by Ot-
taviano becomes a central problem of *The Courtier* and one
that discloses final differences with *De oratore*.

Ottaviano is the one main speaker in the company at
Urbino who cannot appreciate the intrinsic value of beau-
tiful manners. At the start of the last evening's discussion he
argues that the worth of the courtier depends on ends he
serves beyond his own esthetic shaping and complains that
the other speakers have merely fashioned an autotelic being:

> For indeed if by being of noble birth, graceful, charming,
> and expert in so many exercises, the Courtier were to
> bring forth no other fruit than to be what he is, I should
> not judge it right for a man to devote so much study and

labor to acquiring this perfection of Courtiership as any-
one must do who wishes to acquire it. Nay, I should say
that many of those accomplishments that have been at-
tributed to him (such as dancing, merrymaking, singing
and playing) were frivolities and vanities and, in a man
of any rank, deserving of blame rather than of praise; for
these elegances of dress, devices, mottoes, and other such
things as pertain to women and love (although many will
think the contrary), often serve merely to make spirits
effeminate, to corrupt youth, and to lead it to a dissolute
life . . . (IV. 4, pp. 288-289).

In turn, the extrapersonal function he advocates for the
courtier is to educate, serve, and advise his prince. Ottavi-
ano's fundamental criticism begins to indicate the transfor-
mation of roles these new requisites entail. For to object as
he does to the ornamental role the courtier cultivates for
delightful effects is to repudiate some basic features of his
identity. Also the anti-feminism motivating his charges in-
dicates that the courtier must disregard rather than submit
to the demands of women, a proposal that challenges social
and sexual conditions of his existence. Indeed, in the larger
role Ottaviano envisions, the courtier operates in a masculine
world of moral and political counsel. The erotic and pleas-
antly idle relations he enjoyed are superseded by his alle-
giance to the sovereign and, by extension, to the good of the
state. Didactic and political agency require that he diligently
express and apply the moral learning acquired in his educa-
tion. This new aspect of his behavior is reflected in the
serious disputation of the last book, where intellectual and
ethical issues are no longer dismissed or even relieved by
light-hearted interruptions. The courtier's bearing now cor-
responds to the gravity, moral authority, even righteousness
of his new role. The potential power and responsibility that
come with this role means that his previous nonchalance
gives way to earnest commitment. One could go on with
this list of changes to show that the model individual emerg-
ing in the last book possesses attributes much more similar

to the orator than the courtier, as I have distinguished them in the preceeding discussion. The courtier, however, continues to function in a political order totally different from Cicero's orator, and to the extent that Ottaviano recognizes the difference, it profoundly affects the transformation he seeks in courtly functions. Ironically, though he assumes a principality when he defines the political role of "his" courtier, the fact that the courtier comes to share many attributes of the classic orator suggests that Ottaviano, carried away by his idealism, gradually overlooks the political exigencies of an autocratic order.

The participants themselves become aware that Ottaviano's proposals gradually transfigure their original ideal beyond recognition. Cesare Gonzaga teases him for having changed the ideal courtier into a "good schoolmaster" (IV. 36). Similarly, il Magnifico reveals the discrepancy between the earlier definition and Ottaviano's when he says that the latter has deliberately misconceived courtiership out of misogynist spite (IV. 44). Despite its humor, his remark discloses that the lady of the palace can have as little resemblance to the new ideal as would the original figure on whom she was modelled. Finally, Ottaviano's excessive idealism is confirmed in his poignant but rather futile suggestion that Plato and Aristotle represent the perfect courtier he has in mind. Even the sober Pallavicino, sympathetic to the new moral and didactic orientation, finds it hard to associate the courtier's identity with those, historically imagined, of the Greek philosophers (IV. 48).

Although it is not presented in the tidy format of more local debates in the work, Ottaviano's redefinition of the individual fashioned in the first three books constitutes the most prominent ideological conflict in *The Courtier*. Ottaviano's vision of *cortegiania* so departs from the one previously assumed that many readers have questioned whether it does not impair the unity of the work.[14] Yet for all the

[14] Whether Castiglione's book is a unified whole and, specifically, whether the fourth book impairs the unity of the work have been issues of debate in much of the modern commentary on *The Cour-*

disagreement between his views and those of earlier speakers, he reveals directly and indirectly how his aspirations can be reconciled to the narrower conception he criticizes. To the degree that such reconciliation is possible, it represents the most edifying aspect of the book as a whole. But where, it may well be asked, does Ottaviano practice the ideological *mediocrità*, which has resolved former disagreements? Unlike the other participants who moderated personal convictions in the harmonious conclusion of their debates, Ottaviano tries to moderate his views at the beginning rather than at the end of his argument. He will gradually abandon himself to an impossible ideal of courtiership, but near the start of his reassessment, he remains quite aware that the esthetic orientation of the previous speakers can be criticized but not overlooked. Besides, his sagacity about court politics makes him equally aware that the modern prince, accustomed to the ingratiating manners of his subordinates, would

---

tier. Jacob Burckhardt raised the issue when, speaking of Castiglione's Courtier, he said "the inner impulse which inspired him was directed . . . not to the service of the prince, but to his own perfection. . . . The moral relation to the prince, as described in the fourth book, is singularly free and independent." *The Civilization of the Renaissance in Italy,* trans. S.G.C. Middlemore (London, 1960), p. 235. Thematic and tonal differences between the fourth book and the preceding three were observed and analyzed by Erich Loos in his study, *B. Castiglione's 'Libro del Cortegiano.' Studien zur Tugendauffassung des Cinquecento* (Frankfurt am Main, 1955), esp. pp. 201-207. Loos suggested that the last book's departures from the earlier ones were to be attributed to its later composition, and this has been confirmed in Ghino Ghinassi, "Fasi dell 'elaborazione del Cortegiano,'" *Studi di Filologia Italiana* 25 (1967), 155-196. Ghinassi points out how the themes of the courtier's relation to his prince and of spiritual love were successive additions, finally incorporated into a fourth book when Castiglione decided to enlarge the original three-book structure. For a lively recent discussion of the disparities between Books I-III and Book IV see Wayne A. Rebhorn, "Ottaviano's Interruption: Book IV and the Problem of Unity in *Il Libro del Cortegiano,*" *MLN* 87 (1972), 37-59. For just as recent an argument stressing the work's structural integrity and "philosophical" coherence see Dain A. Trafton, "Structure and Meaning in *The Courtier,*" *English Literary Renaissance* 2 (1972), 283-297.

react most adversely if he had to countenance "L'orrida faccia della vera virtù." So despite genuine misgivings about the courtier's ornamental modes, he accommodates them to the ethical mission he urges on the grounds that beauty will captivate the prince more effectively than unmitigated moral counsel. To lead the prince along the "austere path of virtue," the courtier must adorn it, Ottaviano concedes,

> with shady fronds and strewing it with pretty flowers to lessen the tedium of the toilsome journey for one whose strength is slight; and now with music, now with arms and horses, now with verses, now with discourse of love, and with all those means whereof these gentlemen have spoken, to keep his mind continually occupied in worthy pleasures, yet always impressing upon him also some virtuous habit along with these enticements, as I have said, beguiling him with salutary deception; like shrewd doctors who often spread the edge of the cup with some sweet cordial when they wish to give a bitter-tasting medicine to sick and over-delicate children (IV. 10, p. 294).

Ottaviano recognizes here the advantages of the courtier's esthetic talents by disclosing how they can serve as the vehicle of ethical purpose. How effectively he has reconciled beautiful attributes and moral agency is indicated by the idea of "salutary deception," since it allows the courtier to employ one of his characteristic habits of style in edifying his prince—dissimulation. At this stage, however, beautiful cunning has to make goodness more enticing; it can no longer consist of obliquities created only for their intrinsic delight. But Ottaviano's "solution" is not merely meant to accommodate the courtier's esthetic accomplishments in his ethical scheme. It takes into account an inescapable fact about princely disposition and the court in general: moral instruction can only be induced by guiles, beautiful or otherwise. The courtier's likelihood of edifying his prince will rely on the skills he is previously shown to have as a deceiver.

In a sense, Ottaviano never ignores the courtly reality that moral persuasion must appear in the guise of an appeal to esthetic or, as he sees them, baser instincts. When he advocates an austere didacticism and disregards the courtier's graceful attributes, he does so only after being prompted by his audience to assume the role of a counselor so favored by his sovereign that moral counsel would no longer have to be covertly expressed. This singularly earnest and didactic part of his speech is revealed to be purely idealistic by the comment he makes at the start of it: "If I had the favor of some of the princes I know, and if I were to tell them freely what I think, I fear I should soon lose that favor" (IV. 26, p. 310). Again, this continued awareness of the need for "salutary deception" is reflected at one point in his own behavior as a speaker. Not long after he proposes that the courtier beguile the prince in order to lead him along "the austere path of virtue," Ottaviano engages Bembo in a debate on whether monarchies or republics constitute the best form of government (IV. 19-22). It has usually been assumed that his defense of absolute monarchy against Bembo's republican claims is a conventional endorsement of the system that produces courts and courtiers in the first place. But, recently, a convincing argument has been made to show that, very subtly, and under pretense of lauding absolute monarchy, Ottaviano promotes a constitutional form of monarchy in which final authority lies not in the king but in the laws.[15] What is more interesting in this debate than the usual *mediocrità* adopted to reconcile opposing views is the indirection with which Ottaviano proposes that monarchy ought to be tempered with republican principles. For he does this by ostensibly denying the virtues of republican government and by seeming to have overcome any argument against monarchic rule. It is more than likely that such oblique tactics are offered as an example of the cautious

[15] I refer to Dain Trafton's paper "Philosophic Courtiership: Castiglione and the Tradition," delivered at the MLA convention in 1973, and to my knowledge, still unpublished.

and deceptive instruction indispensable in winning the sovereign's assent.

By dwelling on Ottaviano's redefinition in the last book of *The Courtier*, I wish to stress that even when the courtier's new duties of instruction and persuasion supplement his esthetic function, his role and identity continue to be different from those of the classic orator. It becomes progressively evident in Castiglione's book that the political pressures of despotism shape and require an artful behavior quite foreign to Cicero's ideal of the civilized man. I claimed earlier that the courtier's indirection, subterfuge, and deception, so admired by his beholders, were to some extent ploys by which he asserted his social superiority and refinement. But to an equal if not greater extent these tactics are conditioned by the prudential relation he must establish with his sovereign and even with his peers. Ingratiating deceit is not just esthetically desirable but necessitated by the futility of communicating truths plainly. Increasingly one senses that many of the courtier's beautiful manners are prompted by losses that would deny the orator his proper activity: a loss of free expression, of sincerity and fervor, and the loss of direct political participation. Oratory's incompatibility with court values stems from the fact that it is an art devised for a political order where freer conditions not only condone but demand direct, clear, and openly aggressive communication. Such discourse, determined by the need to win the consent of the masses, cannot suit and is therefore ineffective in a system where political power, vested in a hereditary ruler, no longer depends on, in fact disregards, the disposition of commoners.

The discrepancies between the modes of the orator and those of Castiglione's "cunning princepleaser" reaffirm what had already been recognized in Rome under imperial rule: oratory, after flourishing in the free conditions of republics, declined with the rise of principates. There is not much published discussion in the sixteenth century of the political causes for oratory's decline, probably because the same restrictions of free speech that stymied oratory would inhibit attributing such a decline to the autocratic policy of Renaissance monarchs.[16] But a comparison of the ideals embodied in *De oratore* and the *Cortegiano* helps to illustrate why the social and esthetic aspirations as well as the political exigencies of the Renaissance court tended to make it inhospitable to the Ciceronian orator. The comparison also serves to reveal more fully why the educational aims of Renaissance humanists—to produce individuals with the talents of Cicero's orator—were frustrated in the courtly establishments

[16] The correlation of oratory and political liberty was quite traditional in antiquity. So, for example, Cicero maintains in his *Brutus* (12.45) that "the ambition to speak does not arise among men who are shackled and bound fast by the tyranny of kings." The negative effects of despotism on Roman eloquence become more evident and more frequently discussed during the first century of imperial rule. In the last chapter of *On the Sublime*, presumably written in the first century A.D., "Longinus" (or whoever was its author) cites a philosopher who voices the view that the fortunes of oratory depend on political liberty and therefore thrived in the free cities of the ancient world. But present imperial institutions, he goes on to say, deprive men of freedom and endow individuals with no genius except for flattery. Tacitus' *Dialogue on Orators* offers perhaps the most important discussion of the relation between absolutism and oratory's decay. In this dialogue Maternus agrees with Secundus that the most vital phases of oratorical activity occur in periods of democratic and, therefore, more anarchic rule, and he argues (see *Dialogue*, 40-41) that the peace and tranquility achieved under present autocratic rule more than compensate for the previous achievements of oratory. For a valuable discussion of the effect of absolutism on eloquence during the early Empire see Harry Caplan, "The Decay of Eloquence at Rome in the First Century," reprinted now with his other essays in *Of Eloquence*, ed. A. King and H. North (Ithaca, N.Y., 1970), pp. 160-195. About 1500 years after the dramatic date of Tacitus' dialogue Montaigne reiterates Maternus' views in "De la Vanité des Paroles" (*Essais*, I, 51). Sixteenth-century writers do not often discuss the ties between despotism and the decay of political oratory. When they do, they usually repeat the views expressed by classical writers such as Tacitus. See, for example, Guillaume du Vair, *De l'Eloquence Francoise* (1594), ed. René Radouant (Paris, 1907), pp. 148-151. One cause, according to du Vair, for the poor state of oratory in his times stems from the disregard, even the disdain it continues to meet among both rulers and the aristocratic establishment.

dominating sixteenth-century society. I do not wish to sug-
gest that with the rise of absolutism oratorical skills were
denied any outlets whatsoever. What monarchic institutions
did deny were the functions oratory had served in ancient
courts of law and political assemblies, functions the human-
ists ideally hoped to revive.[17] Scholars have noted that oc-
casions for oratorical practice in the Renaissance were cere-
monial rather than political. To be sure, "the humanists,"
writes Michael Baxandall, "took what opportunities there
were for getting on their feet—weddings, funerals, investi-
ture of magistrates, the beginning of the academic year—but
these lacked urgency."[18] The oratory actually practiced
tended to be demonstrative rather than deliberative or ju-
dicial. Despite the humanists' commitment to the Isocratean-
Ciceronian ideal of making eloquence politically effective, in
terms of their rhetorical practice they belonged to the So-
phistic or Gorgian tradition—their oratory more often
served to display sheer verbal virtuosity and elegance than
to sway public policy. Again, the different rhetorical stances
governing Cicero's orator and Castiglione's courtier suggest
why oratory had to become more ornamental than persua-

[17] By the early sixteenth century some humanists recognized the
futility of trying to practice Ciceronian ideals of eloquence within
the political framework of their society. For instance, when, in the
Dialogus Ciceronianus (1528), Erasmus ridicules the slavish imitation
of Cicero practiced and recommended by contemporary humanists,
part of his criticism consists of pointing out the anachronism and
inadequacy of Ciceronian oratory in modern tribunals and council
chambers. "Verum," says Erasmus' speaker, Bulephorus, "ut olim
fuerit utilis eloquentia Ciceronis, hodie quis est illius usus?" ["True
that Cicero's eloquence was useful once upon a time, but what's the
use of it today?"] For the comments that follow this remark see
Erasmus, Dialogus Ciceronianus, ed. and trans. Angiolo Gambaro
(Brescia, 1965), pp. 188-191.
    The efforts to revive Ciceronian modes of oratory were inevitably
frustrated by the awareness that they had become inapposite, but
such awareness did not stifle the humanist dream that eloquence
could be politically and socially effective.
[18] Michael Baxandall, Giotto and the Orators (Oxford, 1971), p.
4.

sive when the political and social values of principates gained
ascendancy in the *cinquecento*.

My aim, however, is not to lament the failure of noble
civic aspirations incurred by the rise of despotic institutions.
Nor do I intend to examine how oratory, deprived of its
moral and political urgency, primarily became an exercise
in verbal stylishness. Rather I wish to consider how con-
genial the norms of courtliness were to those of poetic art.
While the differences between oratory and courtliness sug-
gest why Renaissance courts were unreceptive to the po-
litical motives of humanist eloquence, they also begin to
indicate why these aristocratic establishments found poetry
so compatible. For as the rhetoric of model court conduct
defines itself in contrast with oratory, its affinities with
poetic modes grow increasingly apparent. In the following
chapters I want to point out these affinities more explicitly.
They reveal why poetry could gain strength and status in
the court-dominated societies of sixteenth-century Europe.
They also serve to explain why poets or their defenders
could boast that their art had greater rhetorical effectiveness
than oratorical modes of eloquence in those societies.

Renaissance Englishmen were already aware that poetry
and courtliness shared common features. The fullest expres-
sion of such an awareness is to be found in one of the ma-
jor Elizabethan critical treatises: *The Arte of English Poesie*.
In fact, we can begin perceiving the ties between poetic
and model court conduct by examining how this treatise
correlates them. I will later demonstrate that the preceding
contrast between *The Courtier* and *De oratore* points to
even ampler affinities between poetry and courtliness than
The Arte of English Poesie discloses. Still, the English text
not only offers proof that Elizabethans recognized these
affinities, it provides both a method and the grounds for
drawing them.

Chapter II *The Arte of English Poesie* was published anonymously in 1589, but George Puttenham, who is assumed to be its author, probably composed it some years earlier.[1] This important treatise has become familiar largely through its use as an index of Elizabethan critical attitudes. "Its *disiecta membra*," as the modern editors of the work complain, "meet one everywhere in Elizabethan studies." While critics have shown that many of its theoretical prescriptions reflect and anticipate English poetic practice, hardly anyone has observed that courtly manners determine the viability of these prescriptions. Yet one of the controlling assumptions in the work is that to be a good poet entails being a proper courtier. When Puttenham treats questions of style, he takes it for granted that the courtier is the unrivalled arbiter of style in society. So to make sure that poets may thrive as "cunning Princepleasers," he prescribes norms for their art drawn from approved standards of courtly conduct. This procedure, which I want to examine closely, reveals quite specifically what can already be inferred from the preceding contrast between the orator's and the courtier's rhetorical stances: that poetry and courtliness share mutual stylistic features. And in the course of revealing these affinities, Puttenham begins to spell out for us what gains poets enjoyed from the fact that they existed.

Correlations between poetry and courtliness are assumed throughout the *Arte*, but it is mainly in its final chapters that Puttenham openly asserts their mutuality. After devot-

[1] On the basis of the author's autobiographical references and other historical allusions in the work, B. M. Ward proposed, in "The Authorship of the *Arte of English Poesie*: A Suggestion," *RES* (1925), 284-308, that Lord Lumley wrote the *Arte*. G. D. Willcock and Alice Walker reaffirmed, however, that George Puttenham was the author. See their standard edition of *The Arte of English Poesie* (Cambridge, 1936; rept. 1970), pp. xi-xliv. The internal evidence used to establish the author's identity makes clear that he was a courtier familiar with Queen Elizabeth's establishment as well as with continental courts. For the date of composition see pp. xliv-liii in the edition just cited. It would seem that Puttenham began drafting it as early as 1569 and probably completed the bulk of the work by 1585.

ing most of the third and last book of the treatise to a
repertory of the rhetorical figures that should ornament
poetry, he embarks on a discussion of "decencie," one of
his English terms for decorum. Like "good grace," the
chief esthetic criterion the poet must satisfy, the decorum
that bestows this grace defies any rigid formulation. But as
a way of definition the author begins by providing English
equivalents for the term and its Greek antecedent. The re-
sult is not simply tautological. As the translation progresses,
it reveals Puttenham's tendency to identify his literary
terms of value with notions of proper conduct:

> The Greekes call this good grace of every thing in his
> kinde, το πρεπον, the Latines *decorum* we in our vulgar
> call it by a scholasticall terme *decencie* our owne Saxon
> English terme is *seemelynesse* that is to say, for his good
> shape and utter appearance well pleasing the eye, we call
> it also *comelynesse* for the delight it bringeth comming
> towardes us, and to that purpose may be called *pleasant
> approche*. . . .[2]

Both "seemelynesse" and "comelynesse" were terms reso-
nant with meaning for the Elizabethan reader. But the
comment about them in this passage intends to bring out
their sense of disciplined beauty as it is seen in social com-
portment.[3] And if these equivalents for "decencie" only in-
timate that the norms of poetic decorum are to be found
in the conventions of desirable court conduct, the ensuing
discussion of what is and is not decent makes it quite evi-
dent. For it is not by providing literary rules and invoking
established poetic conventions that Puttenham prescribes
poetic decorum. His examples of propriety and impropriety

[2] George Puttenham, *The Arte of English Poesie*, ed. G. D. Will-
cock and Alice Walker (Cambridge, 1936; rept. 1970), p. 262. Hence-
forth, page references to this text will follow immediately after my
citation. I have taken the liberty to expand contractions and substitute
v for u and j for i in the usual places.

[3] Thomas M. Greene examines Elizabethan connotations of the
word "comeliness" in "Roger Ascham: The Perfect End of Shooting,"
ELH 36 (1969), 620-621.

are drawn rather from representative cases of court beha-
vior. The maker, he maintains, can be assured that his poems
will be "decent" if they abide by the norms of appropriate-
ness called for by various courtly situations. But he is re-
luctant to prescribe fixed rules. His paradigms from social
life emphasize that decorum and the lack of it are as variable
as "the sundrie circumstances that mens affaires are."

Most of the social anecdotes are deliberately chosen to
entertain as well as to teach. Thus Puttenham amusingly il-
lustrates how indecent it was of a French princess, in an
argument about the royal succession, to bewail that God
had not endowed her with male genitalia (p. 267). But in
the next example he points out how the quick wit of a Sir
Andrew Flamock mitigated the indecency of his farting in
front of Henry VIII. Flamock's witty excuse offered "a
sporting satisfaction to the kings mind, in a matter which
without some such merry answer could not have bene well
taken" (p. 268). Here, as in other cases, wit is shown to be
an important component of decorum. It is also what pre-
vents decorum from being rigorously prescribed, since wit
may always allow whoever possesses it to transform ap-
parent impropriety into its opposite. The social examples
lead inevitably to the assertion that proper courtiership as-
sures a command of poetic decorum, since the courtier,
whose social survival relies on wit, judiciousness, and poise,
hardly needs to learn what is or is not desirable in poetic
style. "It were too busie a peece of worke for me," the
author maintains,

> to tell you of all the partes of decencie and indecency
> which have been observed in the speaches of man & in
> his writings, and this that I tell you is rather to solace
> your eares with pretie conceits . . . rather then for any
> other purpose of institution or doctrine, which to any
> Courtier of experience, is not necessarie in this behalfe.
> (p. 276).

He proposes, in short, that, since the "Courtier of experi-
ence" possesses by vocation an understanding of decorum,
he is therefore endowed to write as well as appreciate the

better poetry.[4] A command of desirable court manners, Puttenham suggests, virtually precludes the need for all the literary prescriptions the *Arte* has been providing. If this is intended as a modest disclaimer on the author's part, the idea, nonetheless, that it takes a proper courtier to make a proper poet could not be expressed more directly.

"There is," he writes in the penultimate chapter,

a decency to be observed in every mans action & behaviour aswell as in his speech & writing which some peradventure would thinke impertinent to be treated of in this booke, where we do but informe the commendable fashions of language & stile: but that is otherwise, for the good maker or poet who is in decent speach & good termes to describe all things ... ought to know the comelinesse of an action aswell as of a word ...

(p. 276).

[4] Other Elizabethans share with Puttenham the opinion that the courtier is, by vocation, well versed enough in matters of style not to need any lessons in decorum. George Turberville expresses it in the Epilogue to *The Tragical Tales* (London, 1587), when he hopes that his work will satisfy the courtier's discriminating taste:

The man that each ones humor pleasde,
   as yet I never knew,
Sufficeth if the courtly sort
   whose doome is deepe in deede:
Accompt it ought, with baser wits
   I care not how it speede.
The courtier knowes what best becomes,
   in every kind of case:
His nature is, what so he doth
   to decke with gallant grace.

Sidney's related comment in his *Apology* is better known: "I have found in divers smally learned courtiers a more sound style than in some professors of learning; of which I can guess no other cause, but that the courtier, following that which by practice he findest fittest to nature, therein (though he know it not) doth according to art, though not by art: where the other, using art to show art, and not to hide art (as in these cases he should do), flieth from nature, and indeed abuseth art." *An Apology for Poetry*, ed. Geoffrey Shepherd (London, 1967), p. 139.

So he proceeds to offer more examples of comely conduct on which the poet should model his verbal style. His directives include a detailed account on "negotiating with Princes," which echoes the treatment of this subject in Book II of Castiglione's *Book of the Courtier*. Puttenham can hardly restrain himself from including at the end of his art of poetry the art of conduct it presupposes. He may claim that his courtly readers have no need for social or literary directives, but he still wants to be sure that the would-be poet, uninitiated in courtly ways, will acquire the social refinements necessary for his craft.

If the correlation between poetic and courtly modes is clearly stated by the end of the *Arte*, it remains implicit for the most part. The work assumes from the start that poetry can only be cultivated, flourish, and be appreciated in a nation's most cultured center. It virtually takes for granted, therefore, that in Elizabethan England the nursery of poetry must be located in the Queen's Court. The *Arte* eventually asserts that the language used at court determines the current standard of English that poetry must adopt. But the larger supposition that a familiarity with all courtly style, not only its linguistic usage, is prerequisite for the poet does not get elaborated until the final chapters. Occasionally before then the author suggests that poetic practice is an extension of good courtiership. So he briefly reminds his readers after the opening of Book III that "to make now & then ditties of pleasure" no other training is so necessary as that "which teacheth *beau* semblant, the chiefe profession aswell of Courting as of poesie" (p. 158). He then immediately embarks on the long account of the rhetorical figures that must "gallantly array" poetic language. Most of the last book, "Of Ornament," is devoted to this repertory of verbal devices that serve to enhance poetic style. For the reader uninitiated in the art of "*beau semblant*," it may not be directly evident how the poet's mastery of the figures prescribed will satisfy the norms of a courtly code. Yet Puttenham's rhetorical directives are consistent with the conclusions that follow in the *Arte*: many of the verbal tactics described at the heart of Book

III serve to fulfill the same stylistic effects as those expected from the proper courtier.

To reveal such analogies more precisely, it is first necessary to reexamine certain traits of proper court conduct. The formulation of such behavior in *The Courtier* readily serves to define aspects of model court style so often assumed in the *Arte*. Given the evidence that Elizabethan courtiers subscribed to Castiglione's prescriptions, it is not surprising that his norms of courtliness can be used to identify the implicit ones governing Puttenham's poetical directives. However, it must be stressed that, on those occasions when Puttenham does offer examples or rules of proper conduct for the poet to imitate, he does not draw them from any single authority like Castiglione but from his actual observation and experience of elegant Tudor court style. Nonetheless, as I am about to show, the stylistic prescriptions of the *Courtier* substantially agree with the *Arte*'s poetic directives and the standards of conduct on which they are based. This effective collocation of *The Courtier* and the *Arte* can be taken as further proof of the impact of the Italian book on Tudor court manners and esthetic values generally; it certainly suggests to what extent the English courtly code embodied in Puttenham's poetics conformed to Castiglione's, despite the differences between a large royal court like Elizabeth's and the small ducal one at Urbino.

The Book of the Courtier essentially reveals, as Puttenham could ascertain from his courtly experience, that the most becoming conduct relies on tactics of dissimulation. When Ludovico Canossa recommends the general principle of *sprezzatura* as a way of achieving grace, he makes it clear that subterfuge lies at the heart of it. His initial definition lays emphasis on concealment, since grace requires the artful achievement of being without art. The courtier must, he says,

> . . . practice in all things a certain *sprezzatura*, so as to conceal all art and make whatever is done or said appear to be without effort and almost without any thought

about it. . . . Therefore we may call that art true art which does not seem to be art; nor must one be more careful of anything than of concealing it. . . (1.26, p. 43).[5]

Canossa proposes that *sprezzatura* is at once artifice made to seem natural and a seemingly effortless resolution of the difficult. The acknowledged skill displayed in any well-executed action can only be enhanced by concealing the artifice and effort it requires. This already suggests that the most becoming conduct of the courtier is ironic—his deceptive actions always possess an implication of their opposite. In the more specific directives of Book II such ironic intention is made more evident. Federico Fregoso maintains that *grazia* is intimately related to *mediocrità*, that equilibrium whereby a predominant trait determined by personality, office, or state of mind is tempered by its opposite. He advocates that the courtier consciously disguise a particular disposition by cultivating an appearance of its contrary. By appearing gentle so as to attenuate his martial fierceness, for instance, the courtier can prompt the same admiration in his observers as he does by making the difficult seem easy. He will equally do so by appearing modest in the light of the worthiest deeds. The court prizes and is so alert to a discrepancy between being and seeming that this graceful dissimulation can only enhance the courtier's actual virtues.

Federico repeatedly demands such a discrepancy between what the courtier exhibits and his real talents. Speaking, for instance, of the courtier's musical skills, he says:

> Therefore, let the Courtier turn to music as to a pastime, and as though forced. . . . And although he may know and understand what he does, in this also I would have him dissimulate the care and effort that is required in doing anything well; and let him appear to esteem but little this accomplishment of his, yet by performing it excellently well, make others esteem it highly. (II. 12, p. 104).

[5] As before, page references are to *The Book of the Courtier*, trans. Charles Singleton (Garden City, N.Y., 1959).

Just as *sprezzatura* entails a deliberate underplay of effort, so the courtier's skills, be they athletic or musical, must be performed with apparent averageness so as to make the concealed excellence all the more admirable. Excessive cultivation or display of any talent will stigmatize the courtier as a professional, an offensive quality in a world that is hostile towards all that is obvious and undisguised.

While the observer sees no evident signs of diligence or premeditation in what the courtier does, he gradually recognizes and appreciates the skill that creates his own deception. In the description of courtly masquerades, Federico comments on the kind of pleasure such delayed recognition brings. The courtier's disguise in masquerade must never be so perfect that his authentic identity cannot be perceived at all. The young man disguised as an old one must wear "a loose attire" that subtly discloses his youth and nimbleness. So a cavalier dressed as a rustic shepherd should sit on an excellent mount that hints at his noble status and superb horsemanship. Though the clues are there, the onlookers are temporarily deceived. "Because the bystanders," as Federico explains, "immediately take in what meets the eye at first glance; whereupon, realizing that here there is much more than was promised by the costume, they are delighted and amused" (II. 11, p. 103). Delight results when the actual abilities of the masked individual outstrip the initial expectations of the observers. The courtier masked is, in effect, a figurative model for the courtier in society. In his usual transactions ironical conduct should imply the evident talent he conceals without forfeiting the observer's pleasure of discovering more than he anticipated. *The Courtier* never advocates sheer deceit. If the courtier is encouraged to be deceptive, his dissimulation must never be so total that his authentic intentions fail to be recognized. There should always be an element of mock-disguise in his poses.

The less the courtier displays his expertise, the more of it he is assumed to possess. He must shun long-winded discourse and the tedium of explicitness. His is a world so responsive to indirection that nonchalant detachment may not only imply the courtier's real ability, it may suggest an even greater ability than actually exists. Castiglione is aware that his approval of certain modes of deception may be mistaken for an endorsement of all dissimulation. He therefore castigates fraud and condemns the moral abuses encouraged by duplicity. But his esthetic priorities hardly allow him to forsake dissimulation. Ultimately, courtly grace is inseparable from dissimulation, since part of being graceful always consists of suggesting virtues and talents either greater than or contrary to what is visibly enacted.

Puttenham shares Castiglione's reluctance to provide any strict definition of good grace, his chief esthetic criterion. Nevertheless he recognizes, like Castiglione, that it relies on a conscious discrepancy between being and seeming. As the courtier's grace derives from his various modes of deception, so the grace of poetry depends on the poet's ability to conceal aspects of his subject and delay, by indirection, the recognition of his meanings. Since language is the poet's chief instrument in this process, to achieve grace he must exploit all the means that convey a disproportion between the literal meanings of words and their actual suggestion. The poet must therefore be expert in the use of figures because, as Puttenham puts it, "they pass the ordinary limits of common utterance, and be occupied of purpose to deceive the eare and also the minde, drawing it to a certaine doublenesse, whereby our talke is the more guilefull & abusing" (p. 154). While the author claims that all figurative speech provides resources of dissimulation, his repertory emphasizes the most effective tactics of obliquity and implication. Tropes receive particular attention since, by definition, they involve words used to mean something other than what they usually designate.

The *Arte* devotes two chapters of its third book to these "sensable" figures, so called because "they alter and affect the minde by alteration of sense." For example, the function of the figure *Emphasis*, we are told, "is to inforce the sence of any thing by a word of more than ordinarie efficacie, and nevertheless is not apparent, but as it were, secretly implyed" (p. 184). The figure *Liptote*, whereby "words do not expresse so much, though they purport so much," is a converse means of implication. My remarks on the prescriptions in the *Courtier* should suggest how two such devices can become means to fulfill in words the same grace that derives from insinuation and understatement in courtly conduct. Puttenham rarely comments on the connection between figures he itemizes and the norms of becoming conduct they obey. On one occasion, however, he does observe that tropes have special value because they offer means of perpetrating the duplicity so necessary for survival at court. This occurs when he begins discussing "sensable" figures involving units of speech larger than single words. They are classed under the general "courtly figure *Allegoria*, which is when we speake one thing and thinke another, and that our wordes and our meanings meete not" (p. 186). Before he defines the specific tropes that are "souldiers to the figure *Allegoria* and fight under the banner of dissimulation," he argues that all men, not only poets, can hardly thrive in the deceitful world of the court without a command of *Allegoria*. "The use of this figure is so large," he writes,

> and his vertue of so great efficacie as it is supposed no man can pleasantly utter and perswade without it, but in effect is sure never or very seldome to thrive and prosper in the world, that cannot skilfully put in ure, in so much as not onely every common Courtier, but also the gravest Counsellour, yea and the most noble and wisest Prince of them all are many times enforced to use it, by example (say they) of the great Emperour who had it usually in his mouth to say, *Qui nescit dissimulare nescit regnare* (p. 186).

And he stresses the congeniality of *Allegoria* to the courtly milieu by calling it the "figure of *false semblant or dissimulation*." This digression marks one of the few instances in the rhetorical repertory when Puttenham explicitly con-

siders the value of a figure in terms of desirable and neces-
sary comportment. For the most part the existing correla-
tion has to be inferred.

When the *Arte* describes various devices of irony (which
are subsumed in the class of *allegoria*), the means of making
"words beare contrary countenance to th'intent" can again
be seen as analogous to the behavior considered so graceful
in *The Book of the Courtier*. As I suggested, the appeal of
the courtier's poses often rests in their implication of some-
thing contrary.[6] So the ironic figures of *sarcasmus*, *asteis-
mus*, or *antiphrasis* are specific strategies by which the poet
can achieve the same deception so attractive to the courtly
sensibility.

In general, the reader familiar with the tactics of graceful
bearing in the *Courtier* is constantly made aware of their
rhetorical equivalents in the *Arte*. The following figures,
for example, accomplish effects also recommended in the
Italian book for appearing to best advantage:

> *Meiosis* or the Disabler . . . this extenuation is used to
> divers purposes, sometimes for modesties sake, and to
> avoide the opinion of arrogancie, speaking of our selves or
> of ours. . . (p. 219).

> *Epitropis*. . . . This manner of speech is used when we
> will not seeme, either for manner sake or to avoid tedious-
> nesse, to trouble the judge or hearer with all that we
> could say. . . (p. 226).

> *Paralepsis* . . . used for a good pollicie in pleading . . . to
> make wise as if we set but light of the matter, and that

[6] If the analogy between *sprezzatura* and *ironia* is not stated in
Castiglione's book, it is brought out in a comment by Fulke Greville,
Puttenham's contemporary and fellow courtier. It was incumbent
upon the literary courtier to be casual, that is to display *sprezzatura*
about his writings, serious as they may be. So when Fulke Greville
discusses how he revised some of his works in order to disclaim their
actual seriousness, he explains that he "carelessly cast them into the
hypocritical figure *Ironia*, wherein men commonly (to keep above
their works) seem to make toies of the utmost they can doe." *Life
of Sir Philip Sidney*, ed. Nowell Smith (Oxford, 1907), pp. 153-154.

therefore we do passe over it slightly when in deede we do then intend most effectually . . . to remember it (p. 232).

The correspondences confirm, incidentally, how many prescriptions of conduct in *The Courtier* are derived from traditional rhetorical devices. Occasionally Castiglione's speakers acknowledge that the courtier's becoming artifices are similar to pictorial and rhetorical techniques. Ludovico does point out, for example, that his notion of *sprezzatura* is partly modelled on the *"non ingratam neglegentiam"* advocated in classical rhetoric. And, as we saw earlier, the long discussion at the end of Book II on joke-telling is virtually lifted out of the same book in Cicero's *De oratore* and adapted to courtly needs.[7] But for the most part, since the speakers deliberately avoid being systematic, their precepts for appearing to good advantage cannot be precisely identified with the nomenclature that Puttenham's *Arte* borrows from classical rhetoric. On the other hand, Puttenham can provide a subtler range of strategies because the highly particularized nomenclature allows him to make exhaustive distinctions and recommend thereby a variety of verbal devices to effect what Castiglione's speakers can only suggest by a general directive.

Puttenham's confident endorsement of deceptive verbal devices reflects the important support a courtly code of dissimulation offers his rhetorical prescription. In the context of contemporary English handbooks of rhetoric the *Arte* is singular because of this emphasis on figures that partake in verbal dissimulation. Most of the handbooks abide by norms of clarity and perspicuity in their treatment of *elocutio*. Their authors recognize, traditionally enough, that the term "figure" refers to a device of language that modifies or enhances literal meaning. They also acknowledge

---

[7] For a brilliant account of the rhetorical motives governing Castiglione's courtier, and one to which this study is indebted, see Kenneth Burke, *A Rhetoric of Motives* (1950; rpt. Berkeley and Los Angeles, 1969), pp. 221-233.

the elegance and effectiveness of figurative language that, by definition, transgresses the usage and patterns of every-day speech. But because they seek to control discourse with the aim of preventing, too great a disproportion between *res* and *verba*, they are reluctant to stress, let alone prize, those figurative aspects of language that obscure or retard the disclosure of meaning.[8] Puttenham, on the other hand, makes a much more consistent application of the traditional "falseness" attributed to figures. Whereas the other rhetoricians remain uneasy about their deceptive properties, he playfully exploits the fact that figures "be occupied of purpose to deceive the eare and also the mind." His contrasting estimation of figures that disguise, delay, and conceal meaning becomes evident when his account of them is compared to the cautious, even suspicious, treatment they receive in handbooks of his time.

For example, in Peacham's *Garden of Eloquence* (1577) the figure of *Paradiastole* is described as "when by a mannerly interpretation we excuse our own vices or other men's." In his enlarged edition of 1593 Peacham condemns such euphemism as a vice since "it opposeth the truth by false terms and wrong names." Here, in comparison, is the *Arte*'s account of it:

> the figure *Paradiastole*, which . . . we call the *Curry-favell*, as when we make the best of a bad thing . . . as, to call an unthrift, a liberall gentleman: the foolish-hardy, valiant or couragious: the niggard, thriftie . . . moderat-

[8] In this general comparison, the handbooks contemporary to the *Arte* that I have in mind are: Richard Sherry, *A Treatise of Schemes and Tropes* (1550); Henry Peacham (the Elder), *The Garden of Eloquence*, (1577 and 1593); Angel Day, *The English Secretorie* (1592); Charles Butler, *Rhetoricae libri duo* (1598); John Hoskins, "Directions for Speech and Style," (ca. 1599). By culling various definitions of the figures from these and other sixteenth-century sources, Lee A. Sonnino's *Handbook to Sixteenth Century Rhetoric* (London, 1968) has provided a useful tool for beginning a comparison of Renaissance rhetorics. Sonnino notes in her introduction that Puttenham's recognition of the virtues of ambiguity is original in the context of the various treatises she examined.

ing and abating the force of the matter by craft, and for a pleasing purpose. (pp. 184-185).

The courtly practice of hiding a disagreeable sense under an agreeable expression warrants the need for the poet to command this figure. Puttenham is not concerned, as is Peacham, with its moral or epistemological dubiousness, but with its esthetic effect. By the *Arte*'s standards, the fact that the figure makes a veil of language and thereby conceals meaning is what constitutes its virtue.

Periphrasis, because it is so intimately linked to the allusiveness that Puttenham wants developed in poetry, is another figure given unusual acclaim in the *Arte*. In other handbooks it was seen primarily as a highly ornamental figure whereby a thing is described by more words than plain designation requires. While recognizing its ornamental value, Puttenham is more concerned with the mental provocation caused by its indirection. His stress on the obliqueness that can be derived from the figure is a departure from more typical definitions:

> Then have ye the figure *Periphrasis*, holding somewhat of the dissembler, by reason of a secret intent not appearing by the words, as when we go about the bush, and will not in one or a few words expresse that thing which we desire to have knowen, but do chose rather to do it by many words. . . . It is one of the gallantest figures among the poets so it be used discretely and in his right kinde (p. 193).

Characteristically, he associates the function of the figure with the roundaboutness found in courtly speech, as though its courtly usage endows it with special value as a poetic device.

Even when Puttenham describes figures generally recognized to work by implication, he tends to amplify this capacity in them. For example, *synecdoche*, whether restricted to a word or involving larger units of speech, not only serves as in the other handbooks to denote the whole by the use of the part (or vice versa), but is shown to possess greater possibilities of implication. Thus, *synecdoche* needs a "quick and pregnant capacitie" of understanding when it is used to suggest "by a thing precedent, a thing consequent." An example of such insinuation is revealed in a witty example:

> . . . as he that said to a young gentlewoman, who was in her chamber making her selfe unready. Mistresse will ye geve me leave to unlace your peticote, meaning (perchance) the other thing that might follow such unlasing (pp. 195-196).

Subsequently, the author discusses *noema* when "the obscurity of the sence lieth not in a single word," as it does in *synecdoche*, "but in an entier speech." Courtly examples of its witty effects establish the desirability of *noema* in poetry. Again, his unqualified endorsement of this figure stands out when compared to Peacham's caution about it in *The Garden of Eloquence*:

> This figure ought to be used verie seldome, and then not without great cause, considering the deepe obscuritie of it, which is opposed to perspicuitie, the principall vertue of an Orator.[9]

In their efforts to reassert the sixteenth-century assumption that poetry *is* rhetoric, recent literary historians have obscured the difference between standards of perspicuity in a rhetoric for poets like the *Arte* and those in rhetorics like Peacham's, Day's, and Hoskins', intended chiefly as handbooks of oratorical or epistolary style. Some of these same historians, when analyzing the figures in Tudor poetry, refer indiscriminately to all handbooks of the period as though the rhetorical procedures they advocate were meant for poets as well as orators and letter-writers.[10] Con-

---

[9] *The Garden of Eloquence* (London, 1593), p. 181.
[10] See, for example, Sister Miriam Joseph C.S.C., *Shakespeare's Use of the Arts of Language* (New York, 1947); Brian Vickers, *Classical Rhetoric in English Poetry* (London, 1970). Even in so penetrating

sequently they tend to overlook Puttenham's significant recognition that poems were not just metrical orations even if they had to be persuasive and relied on figurative language for their effects. Puttenham assumed that the production of poetry relied on the same art of *elocutio* described in the handbooks for orators, but he was also sensitive enough to the realities of poetry to know that a rhetoric for poets need not, in fact should not, abide by the norms of clarity that the orator had to observe in order to be easily understood.[11] As a result, his emphasis on the capacity of figures to convey meaning out of all proportion to words is quite original in terms of English rhetorical theory. Moreover, the singular attention he gives to the possibilities of "darkness" in the artifices of language makes his rhetoric much more concordant with the poetic practice emerging in his age. Unlike many of the directives in a handbook such as Peacham's, the prescriptions of the *Arte* are compatible with the view of a working poet like George Chapman, who maintained, "But that Poesie should be as perviall as Oratorie and plainnes her speciall ornament, were the plaine way to barbarisme. . . . Obscuritie in affection of words, & indigested conceits, is pedanticall and childish; but where it shroudeth it selfe in the hart of his subject,

---

a study of poetic rhetoric as Rosemond Tuve's *Elizabethan and Metaphysical Imagery* (Chicago, 1947) virtually no distinction is made between the various rhetorical handbooks of the period. Yet one can already see from Tuve's own illustrations of the relationship between contemporary rhetorical theory and poetic practice that Puttenham's descriptions of certain figures correspond much more closely to Spenser's, Donne's, or Drayton's use of them than do, for example, Peacham's descriptions.

[11] In his *Logic and Rhetoric in England 1500-1700* (Princeton, 1956) Wilbur S. Howell remarks on Puttenham's awareness that different stylistic criteria govern poetic and oratorical discourse. "Puttenham's theory of style," he writes, "in respect to oratory and poetry may be said to consist in the belief that, as oratory achieves persuasiveness only by transcending the speech patterns of ordinary daily converse, so does poetry achieve persuasiveness and delightfulness only by transcending the speech patterns of oratory" (p. 327).

uttered with fitness of figure, and expressive Epithetes; with that darkness will I still labour to be shadowed."[12]

Puttenham encouraged indirection and ambiguity in language because he realized that the pleasures derived from poetry are related to the way it obscures and retards the disclosure of its meaning. I would argue that it was the effectiveness and appeal of duplicity in court conduct that allowed him to insist so confidently on the rhetorical means of achieving ambiguity.[13] He knew that the courtier delighted and appeared to best advantage by disguising himself in a manner that disclosed less than what was really there, more than was apparent. It was an extension of this knowledge that made him assert that the poet's chief skill was to delight with metaphor, leaving his audience to discover the larger meaning of his suggestions. As an intelligent and sensitive amateur of poetry he recognized that clarity was neither necessary nor especially desirable for its effectiveness. But it was the necessity and esthetic success of dissimulation, as he witnessed it in court manners, that gave him the assurance to encourage deceptive techniques in poetry. We almost take it for granted that poetry exploits the allusiveness of language, that it juxtaposes the surface and reality of its meanings—that it is deceptive. In Puttenham's time, however, it took the sophisticated sensibility of the court to value and enjoy what seemed to others perversities of language. Puttenham knew that a courtly audience, so alert to the discrepancy between surface and reality in conduct, could only cherish the same effects in poetic discourse. He legitimates his own claim that the court is the sole nursery of poetry by continually revealing

---

[12] George Chapman, "To . . . Mathew Royden," *Ovids Banquet of Sence* (1595), in *Literary Criticism of Seventeenth Century England*, ed. Edward W. Tayler (New York, 1967), p. 35.

[13] While Puttenham endorses the deliberate exploitation of semantic ambivalence, he condemns the vice of ambiguity in grammatical structure or the kind of ambivalence usually caused by mispunctuation and called *amphibologia* (see *Arte*, pp. 260-261). In general, his sympathies for artful obscurity and covertness do not prevent him from condemning the obscurities of confused or unintelligible composition.

how the sources of poetic delight are peculiarly suited to the courtier's habits of mind and style.

It will be remembered that the analogies between poetic and courtly conduct are made explicit only *after* the author has provided all the rhetorical strategies necessary for the poet he envisages. By establishing that these verbal tactics seek graceful effects similar to those desired in Castiglione's courtier, I wanted to reveal how Puttenham's rhetorical principles of ornament were consistent with his concluding argument. After all, the poet who can master all the verbal devices mentioned above can, in essence, master the art of courtiership. The author maintains that these prescriptions are hardly necessary for the "Courtier of experience" who knows what is becoming in poetry as he knows it in his comportment. But conversely, for the uninitiated poet a schooling in proper verbal ornament serves ultimately as an education in courtly manners. One reason why Puttenham hardly needs to embark on a courtesy book at the end of his treatise is because its poetic rules already fulfill that intention.

He asserts this social function of the *Arte* in the final chapter. Addressing Queen Elizabeth, he reminds her that his treatise has served to pull the would-be poet "first from the carte to the schoole, and from thence to the Court, and prefered him to your Majesties service" (p. 298). The poet, promoted to the court on the basis of the skills advocated by the *Arte*, is urged "so wisely and discreetly" to "behave himself as he may worthily retaine the credit and profession of a very Courtier, which is, in plain termes, cunningly to be able to dissemble" (p. 299). In this concluding directive Puttenham sums up what so many of his rhetorical tactics emphasize. However, knowing how susceptible to abuse his final endorsement may be, he qualifies himself in a manner similar to the one found in *The Book of the Courtier*. Like Castiglione's speakers he carefully distinguishes poetic dissimulation from the fraud and falsehood that justifiably provoke moral outrage. In the Italian conduct-book the deceptions allowed the courtier were to serve only esthetic

ends (though they, in turn, might serve ethical ones). So
Puttenham writes that if natural ease of expression is un-
feasible,

> wee doe allow our Courtly Poet to be a dissembler only
> in the subtilties of his arte: that is, when he is most arti-
> ficiall, so to disguise and cloake it as it may not appeare,
> nor seeme to proceede from him by any studie or trade
> or rules, but to be his naturall. . . (p. 302).

He offers here, at the end of his book, the finest Elizabethan
rendering of what Castiglione meant by *sprezzatura*. It is
a final index of the sophistication that prevails in the work.
But it must be noted that the author offers it as a last pre-
scription for the poet, not for the courtier. Of course the
Arte hardly permits this distinction, since the poet is shown
finally to fulfill his vocation by doing precisely what is ex-
pected of the proper courtier.

While the *Arte of English Poesie* is ostensibly a treatise
on poetry, it is at the same time one of the most significant
arts of conduct of the Elizabethan age. And in the course
of fulfilling both functions the work reveals why the Eng-
lish court could so appreciate the artifices of poetry. They
were the same as the artifices esteemed in the comportment
of its initiates. After reading the *Arte* we realize, too, why
verbally gifted Elizabethans seeking advancement at court
would be motivated to practice *poetic* rather than more
open modes of eloquence. For Puttenham shows us that the
poet, by virtue of the devices characterizing his art, could
satisfy more effectively than other articulate men the stylis-
tic norms desirable at the center of power. And he makes
it clear that, if one is not born to the court but possesses
poetic skills, these can serve as a ready way of gaining ac-
ceptance there. Just as the beautiful strategies cultivated by
the courtier serve him to win grace and favor, so the same
artifices in poetry can help its practitioner secure recogni-
tion and place at court. Puttenham does not jest when he
claims that his treatise serves to pull the would-be poet from
his low station and "prefer him" to Queen Elizabeth's service.

studies in the field reveal that, frequently, the behavior of
the queen and her entourage was nothing less than literary.
Several years ago, for instance, Frances Yates pointed out
the striking correspondences between the conduct of the
characters of Sidney's *Arcadia* as they are shown masquer-
ading in chivalric jousts and the stylized guises assumed by
Elizabeth's courtiers at the annual Accession Day Tilts.
After examining eye-witness accounts of these tilts, she
was led to conclude that "the appearance of Philisides, as
described in the Arcadia, as a Shepherd Knight with a
sheep *impresa* and with his pageant of shepherd attendants—
some of whom went in among the ladies and sang them an
eclogue—is probably not more strange than the spectacles
to be seen at actual Accession Tilts, when Elizabeth's cour-
tiers dramatized themselves as knights of romance, and ap-
peared in costume pageants expressive of the character they
had assumed and of their romantic relation to the Queen
and to the ladies of the court." Miss Yates proposed, in fact,
that Sidney drew the accounts of the tourneys in his ro-
mance from his actual observation of and participation in
these chivalric pageants.[15] Other such rituals actively re-

---

Some other contemporary descriptions of court manners are cited in
Ian Dunlop, *Palaces and Progresses of Elizabeth I* (London, 1962).
See also David Bergeron, *English Civil Pageantry 1558-1642* (London,
1971), esp. Chapter 1. A. L. Rowse provides an informative account of
court life in *The Elizabethan Renaissance, The Life of the Society*
(London, 1971), pp. 30-60. The bibliography on Queen Elizabeth her-
self is too vast to cite here; most of the valuable studies about her and
her reign can be found listed at the end of Paul Johnson's recent
Elizabeth I, a study in power and intellect (London, 1974).

[15] Frances Yates, "Elizabethan Chivalry: The Romance of the Ac-
cession Day Tilts," *JWCI* 20 (1957), 4-25, now reprinted in *Astraea,
The Imperial Theme in the Sixteenth Century* (London and Boston,
1975), pp. 88-111. The passage quoted appears on pp. 91-92. For
another illuminating study of Elizabethan myth-making, see, in the
same volume, her "Queen Elizabeth as Astraea," pp. 29-87. At one
point in this essay, commenting on the mythical image of the *Virgo*
publicly cultivated by Elizabeth, Yates writes: "The bejewelled and
painted image of the Virgin Mary had been cast out of churches and
monasteries but another bejewelled and painted image was set up at

vived during the queen's reign for example, the Garter cere-
monies enacted on St. George's Day, called for behavior as
ornate and theatrical as the courtiers displayed at the tilts.
George Peele's visionary presentation of such a ceremony,
partly described in the following stanza, might seem purely
fictional:

> Under the glorious spreading wings of Fame,
> I saw a virgin queen, attired in white,
> Leading with her a sort of goodly knights,
> With garters and with collars of Saint George:
> "Elizabeth" on a compartiment
> Of gold in bysse was writ, and hung askew
> Upon her head, under an imperial crown.
> She was the sovereign of the knights she led.

But in his study of the Elizabethan Garter processions Roy
Strong clearly demonstrates that a poetic vision like Peele's
corresponds to the descriptions of the ceremonies as they
were actually performed.[16]

Nor was it just at such official celebrations that Elizabeth
and her courtiers assumed literary and theatrical postures.
The regular behavior of the queen's favorites was often
motivated by the conventions of chivalric romance.[17] And

---

court, and went in progress through the land for her worshippers to
adore" (p. 79).

[16] Roy Strong, "Queen Elizabeth I and the Order of the Garter,"
The Archaeological Journal 119 (1962), 245-269. George Peele's poetic
description can be found in *The Honor of the Garter* (1593), in
The Works of George Peele, ed. A. H. Bullen (London, 1888), i, p.
333.

[17] In his account of the queen's court and her favorites Robert
Naunton tells of an incident between the Earl of Essex and Sir Charles
Blunt that shows that the chivalric roles artificially assumed at tilts
and ceremonies were not abandoned when these rituals were over:

> My Lord of Mountjoy, who was another child of [Elizabeth's]
> favour, being newly come, and then but Sir Charles Blunt (for my
> Lord William his elder brother was then living) had the good for-
> tune to run one day very well at tilt, and the Queene was therewith
> so well pleased, that she sent him, in token of her favour, a queene

their comportment, in general, was ornate and theatrical. One need only look at the gorgeous apparel decking the sovereign and her principal subjects (as with their other possessions, the splendor of their clothes was intended to be commensurate with their dignity) to recognize the theatrical motives of their conduct. Surviving portraits of the queen and of her courtiers suffice to illustrate such theatrical self-display.[18] But there exists even more telling evidence: the costumes employed in the theatrical productions put on by the professional companies were often real court garments. "The comedians," observed Thomas Platter, a Swiss visitor in 1599, "are very expensively and elegantly costumed, since it is usual in England, when important gentlemen or knights die, for their finest clothes to be bequeathed to their servants, and since it is not proper for them to wear such clothes, instead they subsequently give them to the comedians to purchase very cheaply." This transfer of apparel from the court to the stage prompts Stephen Orgel to remark "that when the ordinary Elizabethan went to the

---

at chesse, in gold richly enamelled, which his servants had the next day fastened unto his arme, with a crymson ribband, which my Lord of Essex, as he passed through the Privy Chamber, espying with his cloake caste under his arme, the better to command it to the view, enquired what it was, and for what cause there fixed: Sir Foulk Grevile tould him it was the Queenes favour, which the day before, and next after the tilting, she had sent him: whereas my Lord of Essex in a kind of emulation, and as though he would have limited her favour, said, now I perceive every foole must have a favour: this bitter and publique affront came to Sir Charles Blunt's eare, at which he sent him the challenge, which was accepted by my Lord, and they met neare Marybone Parke, where my Lord was hurt in the thigh, and disarmed.

Robert Naunton, *Fragmenta Regalia, or Observations on the Late Queen Elizabeth, Her Times and Favorites* (1641), ed. James Caulfield (London, 1814), pp. 94-95.

[18] See Roy Strong, *The Portraits of Queen Elizabeth I* (Oxford, 1963), and the illustrations in Neville Williams, *All the Queen's Men, Elizabeth I and Her Courtiers* (London and New York, 1972).

theater to see a play about royalty, he might have thought of the drama as a mere fiction, but its trappings were paradoxically the real thing."[19]

The proportions artistic behavior could assume at court are brought out in a recent biography of Sir Walter Ralegh. In this illuminating study Stephen Greenblatt demonstrates that Ralegh sought to shape his whole life into a dramatic work of art, and he points out that, in doing so, the courtier was imitating the queen who practiced such artistic self-fashioning on the grandest scale. Elizabeth, he writes,

> believed deeply—virtually to the point of religious conviction—in display, ceremony, and decorum, the whole theatrical apparatus of royal power. Her gorgeous clothes, the complex code of manners and the calculated descents into familiarity, the poetic tributes she received and the poetry she herself wrote, the portraits and medals she allowed to circulate like religious icons or the images of the Roman emperors, the nicknames she imposed upon her courtiers—all were profoundly theatrical and all contributed to the fashioning of what was perhaps the single greatest dramatic creation of the period: the queen herself.

And a little later he proposes:

> The artificial world which had this supreme actress at its center was Ralegh's world during his years of happiness, fortune, and influence. The self-dramatizing that was the essence of the court deeply influenced his life, coloring not only his relations with the queen but his entire personality. His theatricalism in the crucial scenes of his life, his sense of himself as an actor in a living theater, his capacity truly to believe in the role he played though it was in many of its elements an evident fabrication, his self-manifestation in poetry and prose are all profoundly

[19] Stephen Orgel translates Platter's observation before his comment in *The Illusion of Power. Political Theater in the English Renaissance* (Berkeley and Los Angeles, 1975), p. 5. The original is in E. K. Chambers, *The Elizabethan Stage* (Oxford, 1923), II, 364.

related to the example and effect of the remarkable woman on the throne of England.[20]

Except for the Earl of Essex it does not seem that other prominent Elizabethan courtiers cultivated so pronounced and sustained a dramatistic identity as Greenblatt's biography of Ralegh documents. But what is known about the courtly careers of figures like Leicester, Hatton, Oxford, and Sidney certainly suggests that each, in his own way, also emulated the queen's artistic self-display.[21] They, in turn, prompted lesser courtiers to imitate their stylized conduct. No wonder, then, that Castiglione's *Courtier*, the Renaissance text most fully devoted to the shaping of an individual as a work of art, proved so attractive a mirror of conduct during Elizabeth's reign.

By further attesting that such artistic self-fashioning was practiced at Elizabeth's court, *The Arte of English Poesie* acquires special historical value. In fact, Puttenham's correlation of traditional poetic devices and the strategies of the beautiful behavior he claims to have witnessed reveals to us in a more closely defined way a phenomenon that social historians have perceived on a broad scale: that the code of conduct cultivated at Elizabeth's court was as stylized and artificial as the poetry it fostered. Poetry was bound to flourish, I contend, because the court subscribed to such a code. Although the *Arte* indicates how poets could benefit from the fact that they relied on the same rhetorical devices as those governing court style, it just begins to do so. Bound as he is by the conventions of a traditional rhetorical hand-

[20] Stephen Greenblatt, *Sir Walter Ralegh. The Renaissance Man and his Roles* (New Haven and London, 1973), pp. 52-53, 55.

[21] B. M. Ward's biography of Edward de Vere, *The Seventeenth Earl of Oxford 1550-1604*, illustrates that by the age of twenty-one Oxford had developed many of the artistic accomplishments Castiglione had prescribed. Sir Philip Sidney, of course, was thought by his contemporaries to be a living embodiment of the perfect courtier (see Chapter IV, note 13). One assumes that in his conduct he displayed the *sprezzatura* that was characteristic of his poetic style, as Kenneth Myrick pointed out in *Sir Philip Sidney as a Literary Craftsman* (Cambridge, Mass., 1935).

Chapter III
The affinities between poetry and courtliness are ampler than *The Arte of English Poesie* indicates. While Puttenham recognizes the similarities between the poet's small verbal devices and the courtier's deceptive ploys, there are larger means of indirection at work in poetry than can be equally correlated with courtly modes of deception. Indeed, those figurative devices that, according to Puttenham, are regular features of small parts of poetic discourse can also be seen to characterize the design of whole poems. Aside from its figurative tactics, small or large, Renaissance poetry shares with courtliness a number of features barely intimated in the *Arte*: playfulness and wit that consist of more than verbal manipulation; a tendency to avoid partisanship while offering, instead, complementary, or even opposing, views that are either reconciled or left to be resolved; a capacity for both seriousness and play; and, relatedly, an ability to make instruction, when it is intended, assume the most recreative forms. When these particular features are fully recognized, it becomes even more evident why poetry readily conformed to courtly taste. And when we see, in retrospect, how it did so conform in ways that oratorical modes of eloquence could not, we can perceive why, when society was dominated by the court, poetry could enhance its status in relation to oratorical as well as other types of discourse. Precisely because its rhetorical means were agreeable to courtly taste, poetry's practitioners and defenders could boast of its privileged ability to instruct those high enough in position to benefit society. Much Elizabethan justification of poetry, I will eventually propose, is based on the art's compatibility with aristocratic inclinations and the rhetorical advantage that came with it.

One can begin to infer why poetry would be more congenial to courtly style from some of the specific distinctions between poetry and oratory observed in traditional rhetorical theory. It had always been noted that the orator and the poet employed similar ornamental devices to adorn their discourse. Yet at the same time classical rhetoricians readily distinguished their respective use of figures. In a typical comment about the value of poetry to orators (which incidentally illustrates the ancillary role of poetry in the orator's education), Quintilian begins to point out this distinction:

> Theophrastus says that the reading of poets is of great service to the orator, and has rightly been followed in this view by many. For the poets will give us inspiration as regards the matter, sublimity of language, the power to excite every kind of emotion, and the appropriate treatment of character. . . . We should, however, remember that the orator must not follow the poets in everything, more especially in their freedom of language and their license in the use of figures.[1]

Quintilian goes on to point out that metrical necessities require some of the verbal license practiced in poetry but not permitted the orator in his prose. But when he alludes to the poets' "license in the use of figures," Quintilian has in mind the rule of clarity that must govern oratory but need not be observed to the same degree in poetry. For he is quite aware that poetry can be notoriously unclear. Indeed, in his own extensive treatment of *elocutio*, the examples of figurative uses that trespass the bounds of clarity, and that the orator must therefore avoid, are drawn from actual poetic practice. Whether he is considering metaphor, synecdoche, metonymy, allegory, or other traditional tropes, Quintilian repeatedly maintains that the poet is allowed to exploit their darker possibilities in a way that would jeopardize the persuasive intent of the orator.[2] The demands of perspicuity the orator must satisfy prevent Quintilian from

[1] *Institutio Oratoria* x. i. 27-28. The translation is H. E. Butler's in the Loeb Classical Library edition (Cambridge, Mass., 1922).

[2] For Quintilian's distinctions between the poet's and the orator's use of tropes see his remarks about simile (*Institutio Oratoria* viii. iii. 73); metaphor (viii. vi. 17-18); synecdoche (viii. vi. 19-20); metonymy (viii. vi. 25); epithets (viii. vi. 40); allegory (viii. vi. 47-52); periphrasis (viii. vi. 60-61).

endorsing such poetic license, but he knows full well that
poetry often best achieves its aims by obscuring or retarding
meaning. His cursory distinctions between poetic and ora-
torical uses of figures already suffice to make us recognize
that, if the courtly taste for ornament extends to language,
the attending cult of dissimulation would make courtiers
more sympathetic to the darker ornamental tactics of the
poet.

It will be recalled that Puttenham was as aware as Quin-
tilian (whose authority would support his claims) that the
poet's figurative devices were not bound, like the orator's,
by demands for clarity. In fact the Latin theorist's occasional
remarks about poetic license with figures become a central
premise of *The Arte of English Poesie*. Puttenham admits at
one point that tropes that "inveigle and appassionate the
mind" cannot be allowed in arguments before courts of law,
since they threaten to beguile the "straite and upright mind
of a Judge." However, the poet, not engaged in the urgent
issues of forensic oratory, best fulfills his goals by resorting
to such "abuses" of language. A pleader he may well be but
one, in Puttenham's words

> of pleasant & lovely causes and nothing perillous, such
> as be those for the triall of life, limme, or livelyhood; and
> before judges neither sower nor severe, but in the eare of
> princely dames, yong ladies, gentlewomen and courtiers
> . . . and that all his abuses tende but to dispose the hearers
> to mirth and sollace by pleasant conveyance and efficacy
> of speach, they are not in truth to be accompted vices but
> for vertues in the poeticall science very commendable
> (pp. 154-155).

The *Arte* goes on to reveal why the poet's covert devices
are so agreeable to courtly "judges." For Puttenham intel-
ligently recognizes, as we have seen, that the pleasure
offered by the ambiguous disclosure of poetic tropes is
similar to the pleasure observers could derive from the de-
ceptive manners of the courtier. And in his repertory of the
figures that the poet must master, Puttenham can insist on
those that most "deceive the eare and also the mind" and

justify apparently perverse verbal manipulations precisely because these same artifices are esteemed in courtly comportment.

Invaluable as Puttenham's testimony may be, it is not difficult to recognize without it that practitioners of courtly conduct would enjoy the poet's oblique modes of address. Moreover, Puttenham's (or Quintilian's) specific discussions of rhetorical figures tend to make us overlook the larger modes of indirection and allusion at work in poetry. After all, oblique effects are not just achieved by local tropes in poetry. The larger overall structures of poetry also depend on similar strategies of deception.

Already a minor but distinct genre such as the emblem illustrates how the beguiling effects of tropes are amplified in whole structures. In his collection of emblems published in 1586 Geoffrey Whitney described them as "having some wittie devise expressed with cunning workemanship something obscure to be perceived at first, whereby, when with further consideration it is understood, it maie the greater delight the beholder."[3] The definition can suffice to establish the appeal to the courtly sensibility of the emblem or any poetic form similarly enigmatic. For the procedure Whitney describes might equally apply to some of the tactics by which the courtier, too, delights and impresses his onlookers.

The pastoral eclogue further displays how the oblique effects of small tropes can be characteristic of poetic entireties. Puttenham had himself observed that "under the vaile of homely persons, and in rude speeches," the eclogue intends "to insinuate and glaunce at greater matters" (p. 38). The indirection of the genre is observed in other remarks Elizabethans make about it. Here is William Webbe praising the duplicity of Spenser's eclogues in *The Shepheardes Calender*:

> There is also much matter uttered somewhat covertly, especially the abuses of some whom he would not be too playne withall: in which, though it be not apparent to

[3] Geoffrey Whitney, *A Choice of Emblemes* (London, 1586), sig. 4r.

every one what hys speciall meaning was, yet so skillfully
is it handled, as any man may take delight at hys learned
conveyance, and picke out much good sense in the most
obscure of it.[4]

Obliqueness of this sort not only agrees with that practiced,
of necessity, in courtly exchange it even outdoes it. The
passage suggests that a poet who properly handles a genre
like the eclogue hardly needs lessons in dissimulation—he
can even impart them. And the pastoral poem would be
especially congenial to courtly taste not simply because it
works by deception but because its deceptions are peculiarly
similar to the courtier's. The latter, it will be recalled,
arouses particular pleasure when his actions imply their
opposite, when calculated artifice is made to seem natural,
the difficult easy, the complex simple, and so on. Pastoral
poetry assumes similar disguises: it veils sophisticated and
complex meanings under its cloak of simplicity; it claims
to praise natural things while it is designed according to the
most artificial conventions; in general, it pretends to be very
rustic when, in fact, it is most civilized.[5]

---

[4] William Webbe, *A Discourse of English Poetrie* (1586) in *Eliza-
bethan Critical Essays*, ed. G. Gregory Smith (London, 1904), I, p.
264. Sidney also points out that the eclogue's low and rustic appear-
ance often disguises the higher meanings it seeks to disclose. "Is the
poor pipe [of the pastoral poet] disdained, which sometime out of
Melibeus' mouth can show the misery of people under hard lords or
ravening soldiers? . . . sometimes, under the pretty tales of wolves
and sheep, can include the whole considerations of wrongdoing and
patience." *Apology for Poetry*, ed. Geoffrey Shepherd (London,
1967), p. 116.

[5] Sidney's *Arcadia* is an Elizabethan text that well illustrates the
affinity between the courtly aristocracy's covert modes of communi-
cation and the indirect disclosures of literary genres, such as the
emblem and the pastoral eclogue. I am thinking, in particular, of the
episode in Book II where Musidorus, having assumed the disguise of
the rustic shepherd Dorus to gain access to the closely-guarded
Pamela, finds he has to court the Princess under the guise of wooing
her maidservant Mopsa. In the revised *Arcadia* Musidorus recounts to
his cousin Pyrocles this subtle attempt at convincing Pamela that
despite his lowly guise he is worthy of her attention. [See *The Prose*

The pastoral lyric also illustrates another fundamental relation between small figures and the broad designs of poetry: poems may themselves be amplified versions of the smaller tropes. What is the usual strategy adopted in

---

Works of Sir Philip Sidney, ed. Albert Feuillerat (Cambridge, 1967) I, pp. 153-166]. To alert Pamela that his "estate is not so contemptible" as it seems, he tries to reveal his identity by telling a story—actually his own—about a certain Prince Musidorus who comes to Arcadia and is compelled to become a shepherd in order to woo the princess he loves. Musidorus assumes that as a fellow aristocrat, accustomed to covert messages, Pamela will be able to "read" him in a way that the low-bred Mopsa is incapable of doing. But just to be sure, he reminds the Princess that a shepherd's low estate "is not always to be rejected, since under that vaile there may be hidden thinges to be esteemed." In effect he tells Pamela, "as you read pastoral, so read me." Although in the revised *Arcadia* Pamela hides any sign of recognition after hearing the story, in the *Old Arcadia*, where the episode originally appears, Sidney notes that "she well found he meant the tale by himself, and that he did under that covert manner make her know the great noblenesse of his birth." The episode is remarkable for its aristocratic bias. Like his high-born characters, Sidney assumes that someone of Mopsa's inferior breeding will be unable to appreciate or decipher Musidorus' literary stratagems. He suggests that in literature, as in life, the sophisticated deceptions of poetry can only be enjoyed by those well-born and well-bred enough to see through deliberate courtly veils. Incidentally, in a further attempt to communicate his predicament to Pamela, Musidorus gives Mopsa a jewel (for her mistress to see) whose emblematic device is meant to reveal, but most furtively, that the Princess is the true object of his wooing. "I tooke a Jewell," he tells his cousin Pyrocles, "made in the figure of a Crab-fish, which, because it lookes one way and goes another, I thought it did fitly patterne out my looking to *Mopsa*, but bending to *Pamela*: The word about it was, *By force, not choice.*" (I. pp. 164-165) This second covert message nicely illustrates how emblems or *imprese* could serve to make coded disclosures similar to those made possible by pastoral disguises.

After writing this note I was pleased to discover Margaret Dana's "Heroic and Pastoral: Sidney's *Arcadia* as Masquerade," *CL* 25 (1973), 308-320, an article that more fully establishes how the courtly code governs the behavior of Sidney's heroes in Arcadia and how such behavior helps to define the aristocratic status they are forced to disguise. Dana also convincingly points out that the pastoral roles and general conduct of Sidney's protagonists in Arcadia correspond to the actual festivities and masquerades Elizabethan courtiers practiced.

eclogues? Consider Puttenham's formulation once more:
"Under the vaile of homely persons and in rude speeches
to insinuate and glaunce at greater matters." Or as William
Empson has more recently proposed: "this indeed is one of
the assumptions of pastoral, that you can say everything
about complex people by a complete consideration of simple
people." Such stratagems—alluding to great things by small,
making a small part of the social order suggest something
about all of it—are clearly synecdochic, but on a broad
scale. Pastoral poems can be described then as synecdoches
writ large. When Puttenham describes the effect of synec-
doche, he claims that "it encombers the minde with certaine
imagination what it may be that is meant, and not ex-
pressed." Is this not a basic experience many poems offer
their readers? The conventions of pastoral poetry make it
easier to observe its synecdochic strategy, but the device
is to be found in any poem where, for the sake of compact-
ness and for the pleasure and challenge it provides, the artist
furtively discloses only parts of the whole meaning he wants
imagined.[6]

[6] In *The Rape of Lucrece*, when Shakespeare describes the painting
of the Fall of Troy contemplated by Lucrece (lines 1366-1442), he
praises the beautiful cunning of the artist who made it in terms of his
synecdochic technique:

> For much imaginary work was there;
> Conceit deceitful, so compact, so kind
> That for Achilles' image stood his spear,
> Griped in an armed hand; himself behind
> Was left unseen, save to the eye of the mind:
> A hand, a foot, a face, a leg, a head
> Stood for the whole to be imagined (lines 1422-1428).

Of course, the *ekphrasis* serves as an indirect praise of Shakespeare's
own art. He is after all the artist responsible for the painting in
words. In a recent article Michael Platt has argued that Shakespeare
describes the procedure of his own poem in this stanza, that the rape
of Lucrece is the part that leads the reader to the imagined whole,
namely the killing of kings and the founding of republics. "*Lucrece*,"
Platt writes, "had to be written with compactness in order that no
one mistake him for a teacher of heterodox views or an advocate of
sedition. Merely to treat touchy topics like republics or tyrannicide,

Allegory, usually defined as an extended metaphor, offers a more familiar example of how a trope can be amplified so that it becomes the way a whole poem communicates its meaning. In their definitions of allegory Renaissance rhetoricians usually thought of it as a trope of limited extent, but nothing prevented the poet from enlarging it to whatever proportion he desired. When the Elizabethan poet and theorist George Gascoigne considers tactics for obscuring the meaning of a love lyric to make it more "delectable," his choice includes making an allegory of the whole. "I would," he writes, "discover my disquiet in shadowes *per Allegoriam*, or use the covertest meane that I could to avoyde the uncomely customes of common writers."[7] But the trope could become the structural principle of genres larger than the lyric. *The Faerie Queene*, described by Spenser as a "continued allegory," attests what extensive scale the device can assume. As Gascoigne's brief comment already suggests, the appeal of allegory to the courtly milieu lay in the traditional justification for its obscurity: to conceal certain truths from the base and profane multitude. What could be more compatible to the courtly individual who cultivates a style that distinguishes him from common men than poetic fiction that hides wisdom to deflect the unworthy and to challenge the wits of initiates?

Allegory's possibilities of extension are equally though less obviously characteristic of other tropes. Metonymy, for example, can also become the device by which a poem seeks to conceal and then disclose its full meaning. Familiar on a

---

he had to be furtive, to use 'conceit deceitful,' and to write for the 'wiser sort.' " See Michael Platt, "*The Rape of Lucrece* and the Republic for which it stands," *Centennial Review* 19 (1975), 59-79.

[7] George Gascoigne, *Certayne Notes of Instruction* (1575), in *Elizabethan Critical Essays*, I, p. 49. For various rhetorical definitions and uses of the term allegory in the period see Joshua McClennen, *On the Meaning and Function of Allegory in the English Renaissance* (University of Michigan Contributions in Modern Philology 1947, No. 6). See also Rosemond Tuve, *Elizabethan and Metaphysical Imagery* (Chicago, 1947), pp. 99-109; Judith Dundas, "Allegory as a Form of Wit," *Studies in the Renaissance* II (1964), 223-233.

small scale when the container refers to what it contains, the instrument to its effect, or when an attribute or adjunct of a thing is named instead of the thing itself, the broader role of metonymy is recognizable when it is seen to entail like synecdoche (which it may shade into), the reduction of the complex or the intangible to simpler or more tangible terms. According to Kenneth Burke, who considers it one of the "master" tropes, the basic strategy of metonymy "is to convey some incorporeal or intangible state in terms of the corporeal or tangible." This, of course, is commonly sought as an indirect but large effect in much lyrical discourse. In fact, to indicate how basic a device metonymy becomes in poetic art, Burke asserts that "every art in its nature as a medium, reduces a state of consciousness to a 'corresponding' sensory body. . . . But the aim," he goes on, "of such embodiment is to produce in the observer a corresponding state of consciousness."[8]

Even hyperbole can extend from a small tactical device to become a poem's entire stratagem. In Renaissance love lyrics it is not unusual to find that the author has established a hyperbolic premise that he will then develop right through the poem. The reader is met, so to speak, by an obvious exaggeration that he is asked to accept, with bemusement or admiration, as it is sustained until the conclusion.[9] Not that hyperbole or the other tropes, when applied on a large scale, necessarily remain the exclusive or dominant device in a poem. There may be a combination of broad figuration patterns. As it is, individual tropes often shade into one another. Hyperbolic devices, for instance, are in many cases a particular application of synecdochic ones. Whereas the latter may

[8] Kenneth Burke, *A Grammar of Motives* (Berkeley and Los Angeles, 1969), p. 506 and p. 509. Some of my comments on tropes-in-the-large are indebted to Burke's discussion of "Four Master Tropes" (Metaphor, Synecdoche, Metonymy, Irony), in Appendix D of his *Grammar*, pp. 503-517.

[9] For a valuable study of the definitions of hyperbole and its large-scale uses in John Donne's poetry see Brian Vickers, " 'The Songs and Sonnets' and the Rhetoric of Hyperbole," in *John Donne, Essays in Celebration*, ed. A. J. Smith (London, 1972), pp. 132-174.

ask that the whole be read from the part, they can also demand, as hyperbole frequently does, that part be read from the whole. Moreover, certain rhetorical effects can be achieved by a family of figures, often only distinguished by their size. Just as an allegory is an amplified metaphor, so a paradox is an amplified oxymoron, which, in turn, may be an enlarged version of a pun (when its equivocation is contradictory). Such groups of figures, varying in size but playing similar rhetorical roles, help make us aware of the poet's ability to duplicate in his large designs the effects of the smallest verbal devices.

Once it is recognized that poets rely on tropes as rhetorical strategies of entire poems, the discussion of these figurative devices, like the one found in Puttenham's *Arte*, takes on broader significance. Resorting to the traditional system of *elocutio* to define the figures, Puttenham has to limit himself to their application on a small scale. The conventions of rhetorical theory, determined and designed according to the needs of oratorical, not poetic, practice, prevent him from demonstrating that the tropes have more extensive functions in poetry than their local uses suggest. He does offer one important clue that tropes can be enlarged —when he defines *allegoria* not as an individual trope but as a generic term for all devices where the words mean something other than they appear to signify (p. 186). Enigma, irony in its various shapes, hyperbole, periphrasis, and synecdoche are all "souldiers," he maintains, "to the figure *allegoria* and fight under the banner of dissimulation" (p. 191). But not only does Puttenham define *allegoria* so broadly as to include most of the tropes, he suggests that the verbal dissimulation it characterizes can be extended to entire speeches. "We may dissemble," Puttenham writes, "I meane speake otherwise than we thinke . . . under covert and darke termes, and in learned and apparant *speaches*, in short sentences, and by *long ambage and circumstance of wordes*. . . . To be short every *speach* wrested from his owne naturall signification to another not altogether so naturall is a kinde of dissimulation" (p. 186, italics mine).

This comment asserts the possibility of amplifying small deceptive tactics to much larger proportions. Puttenham does not spell it out enough. Reading the third book of his *Arte* one might too narrowly presume that the poet only manages to dissimulate in proper courtly ways by resorting to small figures. But when it is recalled that he can do so "by long ambage and circumstance of words," these figures can be recognized for what they are: the *smallest* version of the various strategies of indirection and subterfuge available to the poet.

Again, while the duplicity and ambivalence of poetry can be attributed to its figurative devices, these effects result from more than manipulations of language. Just as commonly they derive from the complicated, problematic views of experience or of reality the poet presents. In fact what serves to distinguish the poet's discourse from the philosopher's and the orator's is its reluctance to assert single truths or to plead for a particular course of action. Except for overtly didactic poems and certain kinds of verse satire, poetry is rarely partisan or doctrinaire. It tends much more to be the product and expression of states of intellectual, spiritual, and emotional tensions. Both playfully and seriously it makes us consider concepts, beliefs, and emotions through multiple perspectives. It seeks to broaden our understanding by offering simultaneously or in conjunction contradictory views of life. Just as often it can leave us poised between oppositions it does not allow us to resolve. These features cannot but appeal to the courtly taste for flexibility in demeanor and point of view. I have mentioned how the court prizes the ability to balance and offset opposing qualities or states of mind. So in the give and take of their discussions the courtiers portrayed by Castiglione display an unwillingness to accept fixes on reality that will not accommodate contradictory experience. This explains, to a large degree, their hostility or at least their mocking attitudes toward narrow moralism and doctrinal earnestness. Similarly it explains, as we saw, why they would be unreceptive to the committed pleading of oratory and its usual attempt to prove the validity of single views. But it is not difficult to see that their reluctance to accept unqualified assertions would make them particularly responsive to the complicated, ironic, and often unresolved propositions of the poet. Indeed, the kind of dialectic the courtiers of Urbino are shown to engage in and enjoy—their refusal to choose one view of reality at the expense of another, their testing of ideals against the claims of experience—is remarkably similar to the dialectic so elegantly embodied in much Renaissance poetry.[10]

[10] Consider, for example, the debate on love engaging Castiglione's courtiers near the end of his book. When Bembo begins to advocate the pursuit of spiritual love, asking that men leave "sensual desire behind as the lowest rung of that ladder by which we ascend to true love" (IV. 54), he is promptly challenged by the elderly but still virile Morello, who will not accept such neoplatonic doctrine. Morello quite validly objects "that to possess this beauty which he [Bembo] so much praises, without the body, is a fantasy" (IV. 55). Bembo responds eventually with a magnificent oration extolling the virtues of transcending physical relationship (IV. 65-70). Yet stirred as they are by this lofty speech, the auditors still acknowledge Morello's counterclaims that men remain tied to their sexual desires. Characteristically, the company at Urbino is reluctant to accept a single view of a phenomenon as complicated as love. The didactic created and unresolved here between Neoplatonic doctrines of love and its carnal realities is one often exploited in Renaissance poetry, and I am grateful to my colleagues Robert Hanning and David Rosand for showing me that the courtly *débat* on love at the end of the *Cortegiano* becomes a favorite theme of Renaissance painting (e.g. Titian's *Venus and the Lute Player*) as well as of poetry (e.g. Sidney's *Astrophil and Stella* or Donne's "The Exstasie"). The following sonnet by Sidney reminds us how readily and economically the poet can represent the complex and unresolved view of love Castiglione's courtiers are most willing to entertain:

Who will in fairest book of nature know
   How virtue may best lodged in beauty be,
   Let him but learn of love to read in thee,
   Stella, those fair lines, which true goodness show.
There shall he find all vices' overthrow,
   Not by rude force, but sweetest sovereignty
   Of reason, from whose light those night-birds fly,
   That inward sun in thine eyes shineth so.

Actually the poet's complementary vision can hardly be
divorced from his peculiar use of language. Again, the
broader aspects of poetic ambivalence I just mentioned can
be seen as amplifications of smaller figurative tactics. Or,
seen the other way, rhetorical figures of contradiction and
equivocation are intensified expressions of these features in
the entire poetic statement. For, when a poem leaves us
poised between deliberate contradictions, is it not creating
but on a larger scale the effects of paradox or oxymoron?
The poet will often rely on these figures as well as puns
to reinforce or anticipate the equivocal stance he generally
adopts. Indeed by virtue of their intensity these smaller
devices may prompt greater admiration and participation
in the reader. The courtiers' marked appreciation for puns
attests that the pleasure derived from poetic ambivalence is
not necessarily proportional to the scale in which it is
achieved. Though the poet can achieve ambiguity in large
or small ways, compression is always desirable when covert-
ness is his goal. To minister pleasure to the wit of his
courtly audience, he relies on his greater wit, which often
consists of being able to press large, multiple meanings into
the briefest utterances that can hold them.

The poet's manipulations of language or of perspective
are but part of a larger characteristic of poetry that would
be preeminently attractive to courtly society: its playful-
ness. The milieu as well as the ideal individual depicted in
the *Cortegiano* are constantly inclined to play. Clearly the
poet, much more readily than the orator, can satisfy this
inclination, since so much of his activity consists literally
of playing with words, of making a game out of language.
Nor is the poet's play limited to the contrivances by which

And not content to be perfection's heir
    Thyself, dost strive all minds that way to move
    Who mark in thee what is in thee most fair.
So while thy beauty draws the heart to love,
    As fast thy virtue bends that love to good;
    But ah, desire still cries, give me some food.
                                    Astrophil and Stella 71 (see also
                                    nos. 47, 52, 72).

he veils and unveils his meaning, or to the paradoxes by
which he defies simplistic formulations of life. It includes
everything that he makes up, from the smallest verbal orna-
ment decorating his work to the fictive worlds he invents.
As in any game, the play consists of obeying rules deter-
mined in this case by the choice of genre, of meter, or of
rhyme. Or it may entail playing against established rules,
a conscious defiance of conventions. In his influential study
of the play-element in culture Johan Huizinga tends at
times to be too inclusive in his definition of play; but he is
right to claim that all poetry is a form of play to the extent
that it makes language uniquely autonomous and abides by
conventional and "useless" rules.[11]

Just as he satisfies playful inclinations, the poet depends
on them to be appreciated. His verbal manipulations, his
witty paradoxes require an audience ready to enjoy and
understand them. The cautions expressed in Tudor com-
mentary on the use and deciphering of tropes suggest that
there was a large audience that could not readily understand
language that failed to be literal or was deliberately playful.
And if we keep in mind that a trope may characterize a
poem's entire design, these warnings can be seen to obtain
for more than small units of speech. That hyperbole, for
instance, is particularly liable to be discredited as a form of
lying can be gathered from Thomas Wilson's following
comment:

> There is a figure in Rhetorike called Hyperbole, that is
> to saie, when a thing is spoken beyond measure uncred-
> iblie, and yet is not so largely mente. . . . we must
> diligentlie take hede, when soche speches are used that
> wee take not them as they bee spoken, but as they are
> mente, neither take the whole for the parte, when the
> whole is expressed in woordes, and the parte ment in
> understanding.[12]

[11] See Johan Huizinga, *Homo Ludens; A Study of the Play Element
in Culture* (Boston, 1955), pp. 132-135.
[12] Thomas Wilson, *The Rule of Reason* (London, 1552), fol.146r-v.
Subsequent editions of this work were published in 1553, 1563, 1567,
1580.

Consider how uneasy the poet might feel about resorting
to hyperbole (Puttenham calls it "the loud lyar") with an
audience needing this reminder that he was not perpetrating
sheer falsehood. Courtiers, on the other hand, would need
no such warning, since the manners they cultivate so often
rely on the kind of discrepancy Wilson has to spell out that,
almost instinctively, they would appreciate its verbal use.
Wilson also correctly assumes, incidentally, that hyperbole
is a special application of synecdoche. His warning then
might be equally necessary for that trope when it only
expresses part and the whole has to be understood. And,
again, though the courtier is alert enough to such sugges-
tions, "the use of this figure [synecdoche] is very unfit
among ignorant hearers, whiche for lacke of knowledge may
mistake it." So warns Peacham in the second edition of
The Garden of Eloquence, where the "cautions" he appends
to his definition of tropes frequently maintain that the more
devious ones cannot be grasped by common men. While
he does not prohibit devices of insinuation or equivocation
altogether, he recommends the speaker only use them among
the relative few "of sufficient capacitie and understanding
to collect his meaning."[13] Peacham makes it quite clear that
the use of tropes is governed by social considerations, that
the most playful stratagems of language must finally be re-
served for an audience as knowing and sophisticated as the
one residing at court.

The courtly elite's appreciation of idioms that depart
from or even defy common usage gave Puttenham, as we
saw, the confidence to recommend the contrived and de-
ceitful uses of language so cautiously treated by other Tudor
rhetoricians. But it was not only the deviousness of poetic
language that appealed to courtiers. Their fondness for play
disposed them to value the poet's "feigning" in general,
that is, all his imaginary and imaginative devices. Outside
of the court, the poet could not readily assume that his con-
spicuous artifice would meet with such approval. In his

[13] Henry Peacham, *The Garden of Eloquence* (London, 1593),
sig. Ci. v.

initial remarks on figurative speech Puttenham indicates that
tropes (which, as he puts it, "inveigle and appassionate the
mind") were suspected for their fictive as well as their de-
ceptive qualities. Even in antique times, he writes, judges
would "forbid all manner of figurative speaches to be used
in their consistorie of justice, as meere illusions to the
minde. . . ." But, he goes on (in a passage already quoted),

> because our maker or Poet is appointed not for a judge,
> but rather for a pleader, and that of pleasant & lovely
> causes and nothing perillous, such as be those for the triall
> of life, limme, or livelyhood; and before judges neither
> sower nor severe, but . . . yong ladies, gentlewomen
> and courtiers . . . and that all his abuses [i.e., his figurative
> devices] tende but to dispose the hearers to mirth and
> sollace by pleasant conveyance and efficacy of speach,

hence, he concludes, figures of speech are "in the poetical
science very commendable" (pp. 154-155). At issue in this
passage is not only the deviousness of poetic artifice but also
its fictiveness. Puttenham's reference to those severe judges
who reject figurative devices as "meere illusions to the
minde" serves to remind us that some of his contemporaries
were not ready to distinguish the poet's feigning from out-
right lying. The need to make clear that distinction had
prompted Sidney's well-known claim that "the Poet . . .
nothyng affirmes, and therefore never lyeth. . . . The Poet
never makes any circles about your imagination, to conjure
you to beleeve for true what he writes." Similarly, but in his
own way, Puttenham seeks to relieve the poet of the charge
of lying. He does so by maintaining that the poet addresses
issues removed from actuality, that his artifices and decep-
tions are reserved for merely playful occasions. And it is
chiefly because the courtly milieu both provides and enjoys
such occasions that he can justify the poet's contrivances.

His justification of imaginative artifice exemplifies what
C. S. Lewis generally observed about the Tudor defense
of poetry. Namely that it "is a defence not of poetry as
against prose but of fiction as against fact. . . . What is in

question is not man's right to sing but his right to feign, to 'make things up.' "[14] But, more remarkably, Puttenham's justification also illustrates the court's supportive role in defending the poet's playful feigning. It takes, as the Elizabethan critic shows, an audience like the courtly one, fond of recreation and willing to set aside the claims of actuality, to value the poet's imaginative devices. Such appreciation, coming as it does from the social elite, cannot but serve to protect the poet's questioned right "to make things up" as well as to confer some dignity on his playful occupation. This is why Puttenham repeatedly invokes the court's playful inclinations in *The Arte of English Poesie*. He does so, it must be said, not in order to make serious claims for frivolous activity but simply to assert the validity of gratuitous play. As the passage just quoted from the *Arte* illustrates, the court's readiness to value what are, admittedly, unprofitable and fanciful activities makes it possible for him to consider and to defend the purely recreational aspects of poetry. So the court's esteem of beautiful artifice, as such, allows him to emphasize the methods by which poetry delights rather than the messages by which it edifies. In general, the legitimacy of gratuitous pleasure at court inspires him to affirm what so rarely gets acknowledged in other Elizabethan treatises on poetry: that poetry can serve purely to delight, that it can "allowably beare matter not always of the gravest, or of any great commoditie or profit" (pp. 111-112).

Yet the courtier's and the poet's play are not merely gratuitous, important and refreshing as is Puttenham's claim that they can be. Ready to partake in gratuitous play, Castiglione's courtiers are also admirably ready to use play as a means of self-improvement. There is no better example

---

[14] C. S. Lewis, *English Literature in the Sixteenth Century* (Oxford, 1954), p. 318. "The difficult process," as Lewis goes on to say, "by which Europe became conscious of fiction as an activity distinct from history on the one hand and from lying on the other" has been explored recently by William Nelson in *Fact or Fiction. The Dilemma of the Renaissance Storyteller* (Cambridge, Mass., 1973).

of such *serio ludere* in Castiglione's book than the game of fashioning a perfect courtier that constitutes it. The enterprise consists of a typical procedure in play: withdrawing from the imperfections of actual existence in order not to be constrained by its limits. But unlike many games that reorganize the world for the fun of it, the one at Urbino withdraws from actuality with the aim of modifying the eventual lives of its players. The courtiers properly assume —and this motivates their play frequently—that the betterment of existence can best be accomplished by the temporary exclusion of its daily claims. Paradoxically, the seriousness of their game resides in its escapism. If the ideal they fabricate can hardly be found in actual society, it serves as a model for their possible improvement in that society.

It is worth considering how the motives behind this game resemble the edifying ones of much Renaissance fiction and poetry.[15] Indeed, the functions usually ascribed to poetry by its defenders in the Renaissance are analogous to those of the serious play engaging the courtiers at Urbino. According to Sidney's *Apology for Poetry* the poet also seeks to fashion the possible rather than represent things as they are when he feigns "notable images of vertues, vices, or what else." How can the poet be accused of lying, Sidney asks, when he does not depict the actual? Instead he "doth grow in effect into another nature, in making things either better than Nature bringeth forth, or, quite anew, forms such as never were in Nature. . . . Her world is brazen, the poets only deliver a golden."[16] Similarly, in his depiction of human nature the poet does not imitate "what is, hath been or shall be" but "what may be and should be." The creation of such notable images of perfection (or imperfection) is not mere

[15] For some of my following remarks I am indebted to Harry Berger, Jr., especially his article "The Renaissance Imagination: Second World and Green World," *The Centennial Review* 9 (1965), 36-78.

[16] Sir Philip Sidney, *An Apology for Poetry*, ed. Geoffrey Shepherd (London, 1967), p. 100. Subsequent page references are to this edition.

wish-fulfillment just because they may not be found in this world. Certainly, fiction delights because it carries us into a realm where the recalcitrance and disorder of actual life can be temporarily forgotten. Such pleasure is also derived from the games played at Urbino. But the examples fashioned in fiction, or a parlor game, are meant to improve daily existence to the extent that they can be emulated (or shunned) upon a return to it. "When Sidney discusses the various kinds of poetry," Walter Davis points out,

> what he stresses is the way they offer different potential images of life. Each of the genres, he shows us, holds up for our edification an image of possible perfection or imperfection of existence. A few of the genres—notably the Pindaric lyric and the heroic—are exemplary, and present us with ideals to follow. Many of the others operate more indirectly and interestingly upon us. The satiric, for instance, makes a man laugh at folly and hence at himself, unless he avoids folly. . . . The various literary genres, Sidney insists, present rather than affirm; through them "we get as it were an experience." A man sees himself by placing himself potentially in a feigned notable image of humility or greatness or folly or wickedness or tyranny. He then either seeks or avoids this image in his own life, thus either consenting or refusing to make that image real.[17]

The games shown to be preferred by Castiglione's courtiers fulfill similar effects and hence suggest why the procedures of fiction described by Sidney would equally attract them. For there is more than one game proposed even though only one is finally chosen. Cesare Gonzaga, for example, almost persuades the group to play the game of avowing personal follies. Here is how he describes it:

> Hence, I wish that for this evening our game might be a discussion of this matter, and that each would say: "In case I should openly reveal my folly, what sort mine

[17] Walter Davis, *Idea and Act in Elizabethan Fiction* (Princeton, N.J., 1969), pp. 42-43.

> would be and about what, judging such an eventuality by
> the sparks of folly which are seen to come forth from
> me every day;" and let the same be said of all the others,
> keeping to the order of our games. . . . Thus each of us
> will profit from this game of ours by knowing his faults,
> the better thereby to guard against them (i. 8, p. 21).

An audience prepared to engage in such pastime will be
equally responsive to the instructive entertainment of satire
or comedy. These would require less revealing participa-
tion than Gonzaga's game, but they similarly ask the reader
or auditor to identify himself with and eventually reject the
images of folly created by their authors. And the profit that
Gonzaga maintains can be derived from his game—a de-
velopment of self-knowledge—is the same profit, not sur-
prisingly, Sidney ascribes to all poetry as proof of the
discipline it imparts for acting more virtuously in the world.

I do not dwell on the parlor games at Urbino just to show
that they are far from frivolous, or to suggest that the cour-
tiers who would play them are so serious that even in their
moments of leisure they must engage in purposeful pastimes.
The point is to see from the example of their play the
courtiers' reluctance to dissociate profit from pleasure,
entertainment from seriousness. The company accepts the
serious enterprise of shaping a human ideal because it as-
sumes recreative form. So it must be with all modes of
instruction that seek to be effective with this audience. In
the first chapter I noted that when, in the fourth book,
Ottaviano assigns moral and political functions for the cour-
tier, he cannot disregard the court's low tolerance for un-
mitigated moralism. Ottaviano attributes this disposition to
man's baser instincts rather than to the court's preference
for a tempered style. His solution, nevertheless, satisfies the
courtly demand that instruction be pleasurable. For he pro-
poses, as we noted, that the courtier captivate his ruler's
attention by the display of his many esthetic talents,

> Yet always impressing upon him also some virtuous habit
> along with these enticements . . . beguiling him with
> salutary deception; like shrewd doctors who often spread

the edge of the cup with some sweet cordial when they
wish to give a bitter-tasting medicine to sick and over-
delicate children (IV.10, p. 294)

The simile of sweetening bitter medicine to make it more
palatable is familiar, of course, because at least since the time
of Lucretius it had been used to justify the delights of
poetry.[18] Ottaviano's striking use of it serves to confirm that
the courtier's political comportment must become "poetic"
if it hopes to be effective. This emerges more clearly, per-
haps, when Ottaviano's proposal is juxtaposed to Sidney's
claim in the *Apology* that the poet

> doth not only show the way, but giveth so sweet a pros-
> pect of the way, as will entice any man to enter into it.
> . . . he cometh to you with words set in delightful pro-
> portion either accompanied with, or prepared for, the
> well enchanting skill of music; and with a tale forsooth
> he cometh unto you, with a tale which holdeth children
> from play, and old men from the chimney corner. And,
> pretending no more, doth intend the winning of the mind
> from wickedness to virtue: even as the child is often
> brought to take most wholesome things by hiding them
> in such other as have a pleasant taste . . . (p. 113).

Because its didactic goal is so disguised, "pretending no
more" than to delight, poetry can impel men to virtuous
action more effectively than outright attempts to convert
or to instruct. Ottaviano acknowledges that the same obtains
in courtly conduct. But his transformation of a poetic prin-
ciple into a directive of political conduct is less significant,
as such, than for its bearing on the status of poetry. Cas-
tiglione's speaker is discussing, after all, one of the central
problems besetting Renaissance society wherever it was
dominated by rulers and their courts: how can the individ-
ual exert positive moral influence on those at the center of
power, given their human weakness or, from a less pessi-
mistic view, given their preferred modes of behavior? An
answer lies in the court's and sovereign's susceptibility to

---

[18] See Lucretius, *De Natura Rerum*, IV. 11-25.

beautiful play. The individual must rely on all his talents to delight in order to instruct. How this "solution" enhances the role of poetry is rather evident, since it had traditionally been argued that the specific goal of poetry was to instruct through delight. The important claims Ottaviano makes for poetic modes of conduct can apply to poetic modes on their own. And though his proposal concerns human agency rather than literary means, the value of poetry cannot but be enhanced when its particular blend of *utile* and *dulce* is shown to offer the most viable mode of didacticism in the courtly center of power. In fact, because the poet has always relied on the stratagems Ottaviano ideally prescribes as a mode of conduct, it is not difficult to see that it would be more pragmatic to reassign the poet the didactic role ultimately too difficult for the courtier to fulfill. Such a transference can be noted in *An Apology for Poetry*. For in the course of establishing the social importance of poetry Sidney strongly suggests that the poet has become the only agent who can instruct in the beguiling manner deemed so necessary in a prince's court.

Despite all the commentary on Sidney's *Apology* there has been little discussion of the extent to which his treatise is conditioned by the issues preoccupying Castiglione. Admittedly, Sidney so generalizes his argument that the particular socio-political considerations informing it remain largely implicit. He seeks to establish the universal appeal and value of poetry rather than limit it, as Puttenham does, to an esthetic activity especially congenial to the tastes of the aristocracy. Still, the context provided by my previous discussion helps to perceive how often Sidney's claims are determined by the demands and outlook of the courtly establishment to which he belonged. For example, among the chief claims he makes in defense of poetry is that it surpasses history and philosophy as a moral instrument. In comparison to these rival modes of teaching Sidney proposes that poetry best furthers "the knowledge of a man's self, in the ethic and politic consideration, with the end of well-doing and not of well-knowing only" (p. 104). To prove this he resorts to the old proposition that, given their

baser instincts, men are more likely to be taught by sensory
and delightful images than by the abstract and "austere
admonitions" of the philosopher. It is precisely because
poetry appeals to the playful, even frivolous instincts of
human nature that it can be so effective a vehicle of moral
truth. He does not specify who is most susceptible to the
cunning didacticism of poetry, but the pertinence of his
argument to the problems of instructing the courtly aris-
tocracy is striking. One might already infer that in Sidney's
mind the ruling class represents the chief audience that needs
to act on knowledge "in the ethic and politic consideration."
And, when the author contends that in comparison to
poetry, philosophy is inadequate in implementing such
knowledge, his characterization of philosophical discourse
reflects a typical courtly bias towards it:

> . . . the philosopher, setting down with thorny argument
> the bare rule, is so hard of utterance and so misty to be
> conceived, that one that hath no other guide but him
> shall wade in him till he be old before he shall find suffi-
> cient cause to be honest (p. 106).

Again, after claiming that poetry's delight makes its moral
burden more appealing, "even as the child is often brought
to take most wholesome things by hiding them in such as
have a pleasant taste," he goes on to say:

> So is it in men (most of which are childish in the best
> things, till they be cradled in their graves): glad they will
> be to hear the tales of Hercules, Achilles, Cyrus, and
> Aeneas; and, hearing them, must needs hear the right
> description of wisdom, valour, and justice; which, if they
> had been barely, that is to say philosophically set out,
> they would swear they be brought to school again (pp.
> 113-114).

These remarks show that Sidney is well aware of the aris-
tocratic distaste for "bare" moral discourse. In their own
way, they reaffirm Puttenham's claim that "nothing is more
cumbersome" to a courtly audience than "tedious doctrine

and schollerly methodes of discipline." But Sidney also
recognizes that men will not refuse moral guidance when,
in the poet's unique manner, it is cunningly conveyed. We
saw that, like Ottaviano's courtier, whose beautiful feigning
serves as a vehicle of moral persuasion, Sidney's poet can
entice the reader by the appeal and seductive form of fiction
to entertain lessons he would otherwise ignore. Yet not only
as sugar-coated medicine does poetry subtly achieve didactic
ends. Another feature, emphasized in the *Apology*, con-
tributes to the subtlety of its moral designs: the basic fact
that poetry teaches by examples rather than by precepts.
Too easily overlooked is the indirection devised by the
poet when he transforms a general moral notion into an
example that "yieldeth to the powers of the mind an image
of that whereof the philosopher bestoweth but a wordish
description" (p. 107). Whereas the moral philosopher as-
serts moral tenets and assaults his audience with them, the
poet's feigned examples beckon the reader to exert his
mental powers in order to work out their moral implica-
tions. When Sidney claims that the reader "shall use the
narration but as an imaginative ground-plot of a profitable
invention" (p. 124), he suggests that these implications can
be inferred at the reader's discretion. Naturally there are
limits to the range and number of precepts a poetic example
can generate but Sidney does not propose that it only per-
mits a single, exclusive moral lesson to be derived from it.
Misconstrued in this way, he might be taken to mean that
the poet simply resorts to the most elementary kind of moral
allegory. But surely an audience intolerant of overt and
tedious didacticism would hardly be more responsive to
crude allegorizing where the fictional example stood for one
thinly veiled precept and nothing more. No, the virtue of
teaching by examples, and hence the claim that they sur-
pass arid precepts, is that their liveliness (depending on the
poet's skill) can provoke a range of moral speculation per-
haps wider than the poet intended.[19] More importantly,

[19] Two recent studies dealing with the Renaissance reader's response
to *exempla* emphasize that the fictional or historical example was

examples allow the poet to so disguise moral truth that its discovery depends on the reader's exercise of his ethical awareness. The use of precepts entails moral assault, that of examples invites moral participation of a sort kindred to esthetic involvement.

This aspect of poetic didacticism needs particular emphasis because, again, it so readily suits courtly inclinations. I spoke earlier of the pleasure the courtly audience derives from the poet's oblique use of language, from the delightful hardships he imposes before his meanings can be perceived. There is no reason to doubt that this audience would derive equal pleasure from inferring the moral lessons embodied in the poet's pregnant examples. For in the poet's hands moral truth can be as challenging and therefore as pleasurable to apprehend as the truth derived from his metaphors. In both cases the poet flatters the reader by making him think, while he decodes the message, that he shares the astuteness that went into the coding. It is by such a guileful union of profit and pleasure that the poet affects those unwilling to "be brought to school again." In the course of considering the poet's ethical procedures Sidney reveals that they function as obliquely as his esthetic ones, and, different though he and Puttenham may be in their approaches, both recognize that the virtue of poetry lies in its systematic indirection.

Broad as the terms of Sidney's argument may be, most of poetry's rhetorical advantages over other modes of discourse seem determined by, or at least applicable to, the inclinations of an aristocratic audience. One cannot help but feel that he criticizes philosophy not because it is didactically ineffective, as such, but because it is ineffective in the enclave from which England was ruled. So his large claims for poetic fiction are prompted by his awareness that only

---

assumed to generate a variety of moral truths and that the poet left his reader with the responsibility and freedom to moralize his examples. See Marion Trousdale, "A Possible Renaissance View of Form," *ELH* 40 (1973), 179-204; and John M. Wallace, "Examples are Best Precepts: Readers and Meanings in Seventeenth-Century Poetry." *Critical Inquiry* 1 (1974), 273-290.

the poet is endowed with the verbal manners necessary to promote virtuous action in that same enclave. And this awareness did more than prompt Sidney to argue for poetry's singular importance. It also motivated the finest poetic contribution of the Elizabethan age. In his letter to Ralegh accompanying the first part of *The Faerie Queene*, Spenser seeks to justify the allegorical mode he chose for his epic. "To some," he says, "I knowe this Methode will seem displeasaunt, which had rather have good discipline delivered plainly in way of precepts, or sermoned at large, as they use, then thus clowdily enwrapped in Allegorical devises. But such, me seem, should be satisfide with the use of these dayes, seeing all things accounted by their showes, and nothing esteemed of, that is not delightfull and pleasing to commune sence. . . . So much more profitable and gracious," he then goes on to assert, "is doctrine by ensample than by rule." Despite his misgivings, Spenser knows that the hedonism of a sophisticated public gives him a marked rhetorical advantage. It is precisely because of his cunning abilities to exploit the inclinations of such an audience that he, as a poet, can hope to achieve ethical ends ineffectively sought by plain moral discourse. And, by suggesting that "good discipline . . . sermoned at large" may no longer succeed in moving men's will, he also points to the inadequacies of humanist oratory. Spenser is saying, in effect, that the faith in the orator's (even the preacher's) ability to rouse virtue has to be replaced by a trust in the more subtle persuasiveness of the poet. For he knows full well what my entire argument seeks to demonstrate: that the rhetoric of poetry rather than the rhetoric of oratory is more likely to captivate those high enough in position to benefit society.

One becomes aware that in Sidney's *Apology*, too, the poet has been given the cultural role previously expected of the orator. The absence of any discussion of oratory is striking in an argument devoted to verbal ways of inducing men to virtuous action. Sidney does adopt the form of a classical oration to present his defense but in the course of it he virtually disregards the merits of oratorical discourse.

For suppose it to be granted (that which I suppose with great reason may be denied) that the philosopher, in respect of his methodical proceeding, doth teach more perfectly than the poet, yet do I think that no man is so much *philophilosophos* as to compare the philosopher in moving with the poet.

And that moving is of a higher degree than teaching it may by this appear, that it is well nigh the cause and the effect of teaching. . . . as Aristotle saith, it is not *gnosis* but *praxis* must be the fruit (p. 112).

It is, then, by affecting man's imaginative and sensory as well as his rational faculties that the poet can, unlike the philosopher, fire the spirit to action. The whole cast of Sidney's argument at this stage—to establish the superiority of a discourse in terms of its capacity to move men's wills—is borrowed from previous humanist praises of oratory. And his claims about the poet's unique capacity to impel men to action were ones previously attributed to the orator. My point is not that Sidney seeks to justify poetry by associating it with oratory. Such had been the humanists' traditional justification of poetry. Though in their eyes the poet was less preeminent a cultural agent than the orator, he was seen to share with him the noble role of uplifting society by the eloquent use of language. Like the orator, the poet became esteemed as a *vir bonus dicendi peritus* who, by the power of his sweet persuasion, could civilize, instruct, and reform mankind. Early Renaissance literary theory, as has often been noted, either failed to distinguish the poet's techniques and purposes from those of the orator or deliberately conflated their functions.[20] One reason why

[20] Numerous studies of Renaissance literary theory remark on the conflation of poetry and oratory in the critical treatises of the period, especially before sixteenth-century criticism is significantly influenced by Aristotle's *Poetics*. See, for example: Joel Spingarn, *A History of Literary Criticism in the Renaissance* (New York, 1899); Karl Vossler, *Poetische Theorien in der Italienischen Frührenaissance* (Berlin, 1900); Francesco Tateo, *Retorica e Poetica fra Medioevo e Rinascimento* (Bari, 1960); Bernard Weinberg, *A History of Literary Criticism in*

such a conflation occurred, why poets allowed their art to be interpreted in terms of another, was because poetry could only gain in status by being made akin to oratory, the one verbal art that had acquired prominence due to the promotions of humanist educators. But Sidney is no longer dependent on the secure status of oratory in his defense of poetry. On the contrary, his argument attests indirectly the loss of that status. He not only distinguishes between the procedures of oratory and poetry but also suggests, by not acknowledging the value of oratory, that the ethical and persuasive ends previously attributed to the orator have now been appropriated by the poet. The poet now supersedes the orator as society's great persuader; poetry has become, according to Sidney, the supreme form of eloquence. This shift can be seen to reflect the court's unreceptive attitude toward oratorical modes as it confirms the aristocracy's preference for the congenial, indirect modes of the poet. Like Spenser, Sidney recognizes that in the court-dominated society of England, virtue is more likely to be induced by the kind of hidden persuasion the poet traditionally practices.

It should be evident now why the court's habits of mind and conduct would prove so beneficial to poetry. Its language, we have seen, is shaped by manipulations similar to

the Italian Renaissance, 2 vols. (Chicago, 1961); Grahame Castor, *Pleiade Poetics* (Cambridge, 1964). For a valuable short article on the subject see O. B. Hardison, Jr., "The Orator and the Poet: The Dilemma of Humanist Literature," *Journal of Medieval and Renaissance Studies* 1 (1971), 33-44. Charles Trinkaus challenges modern claims that humanists were capable only of a rhetorical conception of poetry in "The Unknown '400 Poetics of Bartolommeo della Fonte," *Studies in the Renaissance* 13 (1966), 40-122; and recently Wilbur S. Howell has also defied the modern tendency to see Renaissance poetics as essentially rhetorical in *Poetics, Rhetoric and Logic* (Ithaca, N.Y., 1975), esp. Chs. 1 and 2.

those admired in court conduct. Not only would the ornament, the feigning, and the play esteemed in court be exemplary for the poet, but by the very possibility of association these virtues of proper courtliness would help to justify the stylistic procedures that have permanently characterized poetic discourse. For poetry had always possessed and been seen to possess the ornamental, deceptive, and playful properties that proper court conduct eventually shared with it. In fact, the Renaissance courtly code, as Castiglione defines it, drew many of its rules for beautifying the self from traditional procedures in verbal and pictorial art. Though the code itself could, in turn, serve as a guiding source for artistic techniques, many of these techniques had been practiced by poets for much longer than by courtiers. I do not mean to suggest, therefore, that the art of poetry needed the example of beautiful manners in high places to come of age. But I do contend that the *concurrence* of the court's esteem for artistic conduct and the rise of poetic activity could not but enhance the value of such activity as well as encourage it. Despite its ancient history and well-established practices, poetry in early Elizabethan England still had a precarious status. At the same time, that the manners subscribed to by England's dominant social group shared so many stylistic features with poetic art helped to improve that status decisively.

But the poet's role was not just enhanced because his beautiful tactics corresponded to ones cultivated by courtiers. A code of conduct like Castiglione's attests that beautiful play need not exclude didactic purpose. It reveals, moreover, that in the courtly milieu dominating society, didactic purpose must assume recreative form. The Renaissance poet, believing as he did in the power of his art to improve society, may not have needed to be assured that his own recreative activity could bear profit. But because he could instruct while delighting, because his didactic strategies were so acceptable to the courtly milieu, he could present himself as an indispensable moral agent in a high society not

Chapter IV

Poets benefited from the fact that the artifices that characterized their art were deemed desirable in court conduct. Like the courtier, who cultivated these artifices to win the grace of his sovereign and his peers, the poet could use his mastery of similar devices as a means of securing favor and place at court. But even if the court's esteem for poetic artifice might not result in such pragmatic benefits, this esteem certainly helped poets gain more confidence. As I will show in the following pages, the distinctive features poetry shared with courtliness—ornament, dissimulation, playfulness—tended to be discredited outside the courtly enclave. It was therefore a source of reassurance to poets that these stylistic features were cherished and practiced by the English ruling class. And because conduct at Elizabeth's court won the admiration of many Englishmen, these features and other elegant practices acquired some respectability in late Tudor society generally. But the association between court conduct and the poet's art remained beneficial to poets only as long as that conduct did win admiration, as long, that is, as Elizabethans continued to believe in the myth of perfect courtliness.

It should already be apparent that the correlation Puttenham draws between poetry and courtliness depends on a faith in the ability of courtiers to enact the difficult code Castiglione prescribes. Elizabethans possessed this faith until shortly after *The Arte of English Poesie* was published, but the prescriptions of the courtly code, as I will show, proved finally too difficult and too fragile ethically to be observed in practice. Not scrupulously followed, they degenerated into deplorable conduct. When the abuses of the code became more evident (and abuses had always existed) than its proper enactment, the faith in courtly perfection could not be sustained. And when courtliness ceased to be seen as the cultivation of beautiful manners and became the corruption of them, it became a liability rather than an asset for poetry to be associated with it. Still, the Elizabethan poet managed to secure even more social status as a result of the growing disenchantment with court conduct. For while courtiers were failing to live up to model standards, poets, who could, as we saw, satisfy many of these same standards, were perfecting their art. And because the poet shared so many attributes with the proper courtier, he could promote himself as society's arbiter of manners when the courtier lost his preeminence in that role. This transfer of status was poetry's final gain from its association with courtliness. Before considering it, however, we must not overlook how much of an asset the association had been before the transfer occurred.

The hostile attitude normally shown towards dissimulation, for instance, suggests how reassuring it was for the poet that court manners warranted its practice. Just the various scriptural injunctions against deceit suffice to indicate how uneasy Elizabethan "makers" would feel about their deceptive tactics even though these were not perpetrated for dishonest ends. "Thou shalt destroy them that speake lyes," says the Psalmist. "The Lord will abhorre the bloodie man and deceitful" (Ps. 5:6). [Citations are from the Geneva Bible.] "Keep thy tongue from evil, and thy lippes, that they speak no guile" (Ps. 101:7). Proverbs abounds with similar castigations:

> Lying lippes are an abomination to the Lord; but they that deale truely are his delight (12:22).

> The bread of deceit is swete to a man: but afterwards his mouth shal be filled with gravel (20:17).

When Elizabethan moralists cited these and other Biblical passages to support their condemnation of dissembling, they made little distinction between the worst forms of falsehood and the harmless guiles of poetry.[1] Of course, deceit was

[1] Since earlier Christian moralists had distinguished between poetic feigning and deceit perpetrated with evil intent, the reluctance of Tudor moralists to make that distinction could be taken as an index of their hostility toward fiction and poetry. For example, although Augustine considered fictitious narrative a form of lying, he points out in his *Soliloquia* (II. 9. 16) that the poet's feigning should not be

not categorically rejected in an age that had to accommo-
date or refute Machiavelli's political maxims. Yet even in
the casuistic literature of the period, where attempts are
made to justify some forms of deception, it is evident how
little official tolerance existed toward dissimulation prac-
ticed for esthetic ends. The casuists recognize that certain
contingencies force rulers to be occasionally deceptive, and
they will readily invoke the proverb, "Quid nescit dissimu-
lare, nescit regnare." But they justify *dissimulatio* only on
the grounds of political necessity and usually make their
position clear by condemning any form of dissembling that
does not serve public welfare.[2] Outside of courtly ethics, it

identified with evil kinds of deceit. Those who tell lies, he writes,
"hoc differunt a fallacibus, quod omnis fallax appetit fallere; non
autem omnis vult fallere qui mentitur: nam et mimi et comoediae et
multa poemata mendaciorum plena sunt, delectandi potius quam
fallendi voluntate, et omnes fere qui jocantur, mentiuntur [differ in
this from deceivers, namely that every deceiver seeks to deceive; yet
not everyone who lies wants to deceive: for both mimes and comedies
and many poems are full of lies, intending to delight rather than to
deceive, and so lie almost all those who play]. (*Patrologia Latina*,
XXXII, col. 892, my translation.)

[2] Justus Lipsius provides a rather typical example of this qualified
endorsement of deceit in his *Politicorum sive Civilis Doctrinae Libris
Sex* (1589). He permits princes to practice "light deceit" (fraus levis)
or dissimulation that "discovereth the countenance and covereth the
mind," and even tolerates "middle deceit" (fraus media) "when for
thy profit thou intisest another by an error or false tale, which many
good authors do allow and maintaine to be lawfull in a Prince." But
already his reservations about "light deceit" reveal the strict limits of
his endorsement. Lipsius recognizes that his approval "will peradven-
ture displease some liberall and free heart, who will say, *that we must
banish from all conditions and sorts of life, disguising and dissem-
bling*." He goes on to say, "it ought not to be amongst private per-
sons, but in a state I utterly denie it. They shall never governe well,
who know not how to cover well." He maintains, however, that it
would be hard to justify princely dissimulation had not Augustine
acknowledged *"that there are certaine kind of lies, in which there is
no great offence, yet they are not without fault. And in this we deem
that light corruption are only them when a good and lawful king
useth them against the wicked, for the good of the commonwealth.
Otherwise it is not only an offence, but a great sinne howsoever

is difficult to find any sanction of personal modes of decep-
tion, including those, like the poet's, that aim to delight, not
to dupe.

Nothing better illustrates how courtly feigning war-
rants the poet's deceptive tactics than Puttenham's confi-
dent proposal at the end of his *Arte* that, to succeed, the
poet need only conduct himself "like a verie Courtier which
is in plaine termes, cunningly to be able to dissemble" (p.
299). He can openly advocate dissembling because he as-
sumes that while courtier and poet seek to beguile others,
they do not practice sheer deceit; their actual motives,
meanings, or abilities are partially disguised, not totally
hidden. The deception he supports does not aim to violate
truth but rather veil or forestall it for esthetic effect. And
lest his endorsement of deceit be misconstrued, Puttenham
distinguishes it from the various forms of fraud and hypoc-
risy he has observed and deplored among foreign courtiers,
if not among English ones. He disapproves of those who
"seeme idle when they be earnestly occupied and entend
to nothing but mischievous practizes, and do busily nego-
tiat by colour of otiation," or those who "speake faire to
a mans face, and foule behind his backe."

> These & many such like disguisings do we find in mans
> behaviour, & specially in the Courtiers of forrayne Coun-
> treyes. . . . Which partes, neverthelesse, we allow not
> now in our English maker, because we have geven him
> the name of an honest man, and not of an hypocrite: and
> therefore leaving these manner of dissimulations to all
> base-minded men, & of vile nature. . . . we doe allow our
> Courtly Poet to be a dissembler only in the subtilties of
> his arte (pp. 301-302).

---

these old Courtiers laugh thereat." *Six Books of Politics or Civil
Doctrine*, trans. Wm. Jones (London, 1594), Book IV, Ch. 15, pp. 117-
120. One finds a similar exoneration of princely deceit or "policy" in
the Protestant casuistry of William Perkins, perhaps the most popular
English preacher at the end of the sixteenth century. For a discussion
of Perkins' treatment of lying and deceit see George L. Mosse, *The
Holy Pretense, A Study in Christianity and Reason of State from
William Perkins to John Winthrop* (Oxford, 1957), esp. pp. 48-68.

By so endorsing dissimulation while recognizing its likely abuses, Puttenham affirms both his faith in the possibility of proper courtliness and his esteem for beautiful manners. Like Castiglione's speakers, he knows that the fulfillment of proper style depends on a discrepancy between being and seeming and therefore invites, even if it does not permit, immoral practices. But like them, too, he is willing to take the ethical chance of sanctioning dissimulation because he has faith that the courtier and the poet will resort to deception only for esthetic appeal. As a devotee of graceful style he considers it too precious to forfeit just because its tactics skirt perilously close to moral transgression. This is where he significantly differs from contemporary and more puritanical moralists who did not deem esthetic pleasure worth the risk of permitting the deceptive means it might require. He, on the other hand, prizes such pleasure enough to believe that the beautiful effects achieved by deception compensate for its ethical fragility.

The drawback, however, is that such ethical fragility does not disappear simply by being recognized. Even while distinguishing between beautiful cunning and the deceits of "base-minded men," Puttenham makes us all the more aware of the thin line that separates them. Too little prevents the approved forms of deception from degenerating into outright vice. And when actually practiced, it appears that the courtly cult of dissimulation did not just border on ethical transgressions but tended to lapse into them. Tudor anti-courtly criticism reminds us that, in contrast to its beautiful aspirations, courtly style also consisted of deplorable abuses; the condemnation of deceit and falsehood in that criticism indicates that what Puttenham dismisses as foreign aberrations were as likely to be the norm among English courtiers. Although anti-courtly critics tend to exaggerate the vices of court style just as its proponents idealize its virtues, it is obvious that not every courtier could be a "Courtier." Some were bound to violate the delicate sanction of dissimulation in their inept attempts to be fashionable. Even worse, some could use the sanction to commit any kind of duplicity that might forward their dishonest ends. The

moral injunctions against sheer deceit included in the code
would not suffice to prevent the subterfuge it encourages
from lapsing into imposture and fraud.

Abuses are bound to be encouraged by the cult of dis-
simulation. But deceit and hypocrisy are only the most evi-
dent afflictions that courtly esthetics help to engender. All
the stylistic attributes that beautify conduct and that ac-
quire respectability by being cultivated in high places are,
at the same time, closely linked to the corrupt manners tra-
ditionally deplored by the critics of court morals. Consider
the value courtiers placed on ornamentation. As I showed
earlier, this predilection for ornament, reflected by the
approval of all behavior that refines, obscures, exaggerates,
and in short departs from common usage, would make
courtiers sympathetic to the poet's embellishment of lan-
guage. Conversely, Elizabethans of plainer taste, intolerant
of verbal adornment, were prone to criticize "sugared sen-
tences," "filed speech," "elegancie of phrase," and the
"vain affectation of eloquence" generally.[3] More severe
Tudor critics of art's corruptions—who often aired their
views in diatribes against cosmetics and gorgeousness of ap-
parel—condemned ornament as a perverse attempt to trans-
form man's natural attributes as well as God's workman-
ship. Probably the best known attack against such ornament
was "The Sermon Against Excess of Apparel" included in
the *Homilies* repeatedly read in Elizabethan churches.
"Who can paynt her face," the sermon proclaims,

> and curle her heere, and chaunge it to an unnaturall col-
> oure, but therein doth worke reprofe to her maker, who
> made her? As though she could make her selfe more
> comely, than GOD hath appoynted the measure of her
> beautie. What do these women, but go about to refourme
> that whiche God hath made? not knowing that all thinges

[3] Many of the Tudor critics who inveigh against verbal ornament
and the "vain affectation of eloquence" are cited in R. F. Jones, "The
Moral Sense of Simplicity," *Studies in Honor of Frederick Shipley*
(St. Louis, 1942), pp. 265-287.

naturall, is the worke of God: and thynges disguysed, unnaturall be the workes of the devyll.[4]

Anti-ornamental attitudes also often disguised anti-courtly ones. The link between them is brought out in this reproach from a contemporary sermon:

> Some thinke Christ too homely and playne for them, and not gallant ynough to maintayne them in their pride, in their great ruffes, gorbellies, broadred heare, and a thousand such vanities which hinder them from matching with Christ. The courtlike minions drowned in their pleasures are ashamed of the playnnes of Christ, for they that are in kinges' houses weare soft apparell, but Christ is without such pompe.[5]

With such hostile sentiments existing in the culture, the poet could only be relieved to find that in the courtly enclave the same sort of ornament he used to adorn language was cultivated with devotion. But, again, devotion led to

---

[4] *The second tome of homelyes* (London, 1563), p. 117v. At least twelve editions were printed by 1595.

[5] Bartimeus Andrewes, *Certaine verie worthie sermons upon the fifth chapter of the Songs of Solomon* (London, 1583), sig. C 6v. In comparison to such anti-ornamental harangue consider Puttenham's comment on the relation between the gorgeousness of court dress and the poet's verbal ornaments:

> And as we see in these great Madames of honour, be they for personage or otherwise never so comely and bewtifull, yet if they want their courtly habillements or at leastwise such other apparell as custome and civilitie have ordained to cover their naked bodies, would be halfe ashamed or greatly out of countenaunce to be seen in that sort, and perchance do then thinke themselves more amiable in every mans eye, when they be in their richest attire, suppose of silkes or tyssewes & costly embroderies, then when they go in cloth or in any other plaine and simple apparell. Even so cannot our vulgar Poesie shew it selfe either gallant or gorgious, if any lymme be left naked, and bare and not clad in his kindly clothes and colours, such as may convey them somwhat out of sight, that is from the common course of ordinary speach and capacitie of the vulgar judgement, and yet being artificially handled must needes yeld it more bewtie and commendation (*Arte*, pp. 137-138).

abuse. By advocating departures from common usage as means of beautifying conduct, the courtly code was unable to prevent the hollow artificiality and affectation satirized by the court's critics. If the example of the proper courtier, beautifying nature by art, helped to refute the detractors of all artifice, the more likely evidence of fops, distorting nature's endowments, could provide living proof that ornament was perverse falsification. Ornamental display, like dissimulation, was liable to be perverted by unscrupulous courtiers. And the violation of such esthetic procedures in court conduct threatened to further discredit rather than enhance them.

What holds true for ornamental display applies equally to courtly playfulness. Again, we must not forget how supportive the courtly esteem of play could prove to the poet faced with the hostile attitudes to recreation officially prevailing in his society. Poetic entertainments, like other recreative activities, were open to charges of uselessness, idleness, and escapism by Englishmen committed to the work ethic or the more stringest rules of Christian morality.[6] On the other hand, the court's preference for recrea-

[6] William Perkins' influential casuistry offers a good example of the official Protestant "position" on recreation in Elizabethan times. Consider how difficult it would be for poets to justify their playful motives when the recreation of the righteous Christian had to abide by directives such as the following:

Our Recreations must be profitable to our selves and others; and they must tend also to the glory of God. Our Saviour Christ sayes, *that of every idle word that men shall speake, they shall give an account at the day of judgement*, Mat.12.36. Where by *idle words*, he meaneth such, as bring no profit to men, nor honour to God. And if for idle words, then also for idle recreations, must we be accountable to him. . . . the scope and end of all recreations is, that God may be honoured in and by them. . . .

Now Recreation must be sparing, two waies.

First in regard of *time*. For we must redeeme the time, that is, take time while time lasteth, for the procuring of life everlasting. Eph. 5.16. This condemneth the wicked practice of many men, that follow this game and that, to drive away time, whereas they should employ all the time that they do, to doe Gods will. . . .

Secondly, Recreation must be sparing in regard *of our affection.*

tive forms of instruction, its appreciation of the constructive values of escapism served to offset these charges. Aside from affirming the moral or didactic value of recreation courtiers enhanced all modes of it by their tolerance of gratuitous play, their contempt for the merely useful, and their distaste for unrelieved seriousness. Once again, though, the courtier's playful impulses were liable to degenerate. Conditioned by leisure, itself the consequence of restricted political activity, such impulses could lead to trivial and purely idle amusement. Take, for example, the courtier's fondness for jokes and his readiness to make them, traits that reflect his distaste for unrelieved seriousness. At its best, such an aversion prompts the courtier to be facetious while being serious, thereby offsetting gravity and making it more engaging. Blended with earnestness, humor becomes another means of displaying his rightly admired capacity to embody opposites. And to the extent that the courtly code shows how this complex blend of earnestness and levity does not jeopardize seriousness but renders it more attractive, it helps to validate, in turn, the poet's frequent practice of *serio ludere*. At its worst, however, the courtly intolerance of sheer didacticism encourages pointless joking, fatuous levity, and a philistine disregard of intellectual or ethical issues. It takes little for the delicate blend of seriousness and play to lapse into the worst kind of shallowness. On the pretext that elegance calls for serious matters to be treated gamesomely, the courtly fop will simply trivialize them. In general, when not governed by the principles of a difficult code like Castiglione's, the courtier's play can become abject proof of his parasitic, frivolous existence. And by being associated with such pastimes, poetry risks being criticized as an equally frivolous activity.

A feature of court behavior that I have not considered

For we may not set our hearts upon sports, but our affection must be tempered and allaied with the feare of God. . . .

From Book III, Ch. iv., section 4 of *The Whole Treatise of Cases of Conscience* (London, 1608) reprinted in *William Perkins 1558-1602, English Puritanist*, ed. Thomas Merrill (Nieuwkoop, 1966), p. 222.

but that also invites and encourages poetic talent is the
necessity to compliment and flatter. Like the other stylistic
aspects of courtliness beneficial for poetry, it is ethically
problematic, perhaps even more so than the rest. The hom-
age the sovereign demands of his subjects, the pursuit and
preservation of royal favor, make compliments imperative
in the courtier's transactions with his prince. And since the
relationship between prince and courtier equally obtains be-
tween the courtier and inferiors seeking his grace, praise
has to be lavished not only on the sovereign but on those
who enjoy his favor. The praise made necessary by such
hierarchal relations cannot be disinterested; more often it
is bestowed for political motives rather than for the actual
worth of its recipients. As a result, flattery is inevitable.
And it hardly needs saying that flattery is decried as the
most pernicious of courtly vices. At their worst, flatterers
so pervert the truth that they encourage rulers to indulge
in vices by praising them as virtues. At best, they exaggerate
the truth by bestowing praise hardly warranted by the
merit of their object. Yet the court's encomiastic needs,
stemming from the very conditions that foster a scourge
like flattery, create employment for poets whose original
functions are, after all, to praise and celebrate. The pen-
chant for festive celebration, pageantry, and praise in the
royal establishment made the poet's epideictic skills one of
his most prized abilities. One need only bear in mind the
number of poetic genres based on eulogistic principles—for
example, the hymn, the epic, the ode, the elegy, the epitha-
lamion, the epigram—to appreciate how the numerous occa-
sions that call for praise of the sovereign or the court's
great persons can offer the poet opportunities of work.

Again, though, this aspect of courtliness that stimulates
poetic expression is also responsible for the existence of
offensive conduct. Even more disturbing, it is hard to dis-
tinguish the excessive praise in the panegyrics the poet is
commissioned to produce (or which he independently
composes for his own advancement) from quite abject
flattery. Only the conventions of epideictic discourse allow

the poet to dissociate his lying praise from that of the flatterer. For, ever since Aristotle's *Rhetoric* had permitted some discrepancy between the heightened praise of a person and his actual attributes, literary flattery had been sanctioned by rhetorical theorists as a means of inspiring virtue. Such flattery was defended on the grounds that it incited either the person praised or others appreciating the praise to emulate the ideal projected in the oratorical or poetic encomium. "No other way of correcting a prince," Erasmus maintains, "is so efficacious as presenting, in the guise of flattery, the pattern of a really good prince."[7] Like deception, then, flattery could be justified by poets (or courtiers) as a necessary manipulation of truth serving to disguise ethical lessons that would not be entertained if plainly delivered. Still, such clever distinctions between the poet's exaggerated praise and servile flattery do not genuinely resolve the ethical issue. Poets deceive and flatter. By these dubious methods they produce beautiful artifacts. Although they do not resort to such tactics for malevolent ends, they benefit from the conditions that foster deplorable habits like hypocrisy, fraud, and fawning ambition.

In Chapter I, when discussing the difference between Cicero's and Castiglione's ideals of the civilized man, I proposed that the esthetics of the courtly code were shaped by the political pressures of despotism as much as by the social habits and tastes of the aristocracy. Indirection and subterfuge, for instance, are tactics not only stylistically becoming but necessary for political survival in a world where plain, direct communication is perilous. But if the

[7] See Aristotle, *Rhetoric* I. ix; Erasmus' remark can be found in *Opus Epistolarum Erasmi*, ed., P. S. Allen (Oxford, 1906), I, 397. Similarly, to justify his excessive praises of different patronesses, John Donne remarked to Lady Herbert that "of the greatest flattery there is this good use, that they tell us what we should be." For further discussion of the traditional justification of excessive literary praise see O. B. Hardison, Jr., *The Enduring Monument. A Study of the Idea of Praise in Renaissance Literary Theory and Practice* (Chapel Hill, 1962), esp. pp. 31-32; and Barbara Lewalski, *Donne's Anniversaries and the Poetry of Praise* (Princeton, 1973), pp. 16-19.

political and social exigencies of an autocratic order compel the good courtier to resort to beautiful dissimulation, they also motivate less scrupulous courtiers to be treacherously guileful. The causes that warrant "salutary deception" also motivate lying and hypocrisy. And if for these same causes playful and encomiastic methods become desirable means of communicating truth, so because of them frivolity and flattery emerge as menaces. Despotism imposes stylistic norms that at once encourage beautiful modes of expression and ethical transgressions. The favorable conditions such a political system provides for art also invite the moral corruption that threatens it. Obviously if princes and their courtiers could contemplate truth not elegantly dressed, unattentuated, or unheightened, there would be less room for flattery and pernicious deceit. But there would be equally less appreciation or need for the poet's beautiful deviousness.

The very aspects of court style that helped make certain poetic practices respectable are barely separable from vices that afflict despotic institutions. This fragile distinction between the courtier's model conduct and the offensive behavior bound to coexist with it ultimately makes the association between poetry and courtliness equally fragile. When the abuses of proper court style, inevitable in actual practice, predominate over exemplary politeness, poets can only suffer further discredit by being associated with courtly manners. The dissociation becomes all the more pressing since the abuses themselves bear too close a resemblance to the poet's own stylistic processes and may be wrongly confused with legitimate artistic means. On the other hand, it should now be more evident that the correlation of poetry and courtliness depends on a faith in the ability of courtiers to approximate the conduct Castiglione prescribed. Puttenham displays this faith in the *Arte of English Poesie*. It allows him, for instance, to call upon the poet to dissemble "like a verie Courtier." In general, without such faith he could not advise poets to emulate the stylistic accomplishment of Elizabeth's courtiers. Of course, by celebrating this accomplishment, the *Arte* itself makes a significant contribution to the Elizabethan myth of courtly perfection. But Puttenham is by no means alone in subscribing to this myth. Many of his contemporaries, at least until the 1590s, shared his respect for the social and stylistic authority of Elizabeth's court. And, as I am about to show, for most of the queen's reign even anti-courtly literature displayed a faith in the court's perfectability. As long as Elizabethans espoused the myth of the perfect courtier, so long did the court's stylistic norms play a significant role in enhancing poetic practice. By the last decade of the century, when their faith could no longer be sustained, the relation of poets and courtiers becomes radically altered but not, we will see, immediately severed.

When Elizabethan moralists condemn courtly abuses, they often extol, at the very same time, the admirable conduct of their queen and her circle of courtiers. This peculiar ambivalence that characterizes English criticism of the court between 1560 and 1590 offers perhaps the best index of a persistent Elizabethan belief in the myth of perfect courtliness. It also helps to distinguish Elizabethan anti-courtly sentiments from those expressed earlier in the century, especially during Henry VIII's reign. Admittedly, all Tudor critics of court manners often reiterated traditional complaints about the *aulica vita* already found in classical and medieval sources. Nonetheless, the fact that Elizabethan writers relied on moralistic commonplaces when condemning courtly ways must not be allowed to obscure the fact that their objections tended to be more reserved than the complaints expressed, say, by Skelton, More, and Wyatt.[8]

[8] For a thorough survey of anti-courtly literature in medieval and Renaissance England see Claus Uhlig, *Hofkritik im England des Mittelalters und der Renaissance* (Berlin, 1973). Intent on showing that anti-courtly literature belongs to a tradition of moralistic commonplaces, Professor Uhlig insists on sameness rather than difference

Not that these earlier Tudor critics failed to qualify their strictures as well when they vilified the court. But their ambivalent attitudes stemmed primarily from their commitment to the humanist ideal of public service (which had to be fulfilled at court, its pitfalls notwithstanding). During Elizabeth's reign, however, more than the humanist dream of political service prompted court critics to qualify their complaints. First of all, their anti-courtly attitudes were modified by the growing pride they shared with other Englishmen in their nation and the monarchic institution governing it.

So, in the traditional criticism of princely establishments as nurseries of vice, one finds that Elizabethans level their accusations at foreign courts rather than their queen's, which they often praise for its unique and exemplary virtues. It will be recalled that, when Puttenham himself acknowledges the likelihood of courtly abuses, he maintains that he has only witnessed them abroad. The same sort of chauvinism can be found in an earlier document, William Harrison's *Description of England* (1577, 1587). "In some great princes' courts beyond the seas," writes Harrison, when he describes Elizabeth's royal establishment,

> . . . it is a world to see what lewd behavior is used among divers of those that resort unto the same, and what whoredom, swearing, rivalry, atheism, dicing, carding, carousing, drunkenness, gluttony, quarreling, and such like inconveniences do daily take hold, and sometimes even among those in whose estates the like behavior is least convenient (whereby their talk is verified which say that everything increaseth and groweth in the courts of princes saving virtue, which in such places doth languish and daily fade away), all which enormities are either utterly expelled out of the court of England or else so

in his survey. He does, however, recognize, if somewhat reluctantly, that a number of Elizabethan critics condemn courtly manners while praising the admirable conduct of their queen and her circle of courtiers.

qualified by the diligent endeavor of the chief officers of Her Grace's household that seldom are any of these things apparently seen there without due reprehension and such severe correction as belongeth to those trespasses.[9]

Elizabeth's court is not always so exonerated. The actual, observed misconduct of her courtiers is occasionally criticized; but the aristocratic values that may have determined such misconduct remain intact. Restricting themselves to a denunciation of individual abuses and excesses, the critics of the court prescribe as a remedy to these abuses a pattern of conduct based on courtly aspirations. The imperfections are condemned insofar as they violate the rules embodied in the courtly code. By proposing moral and social improvements that derive from the code itself, these critics confirm the vitality of the myth of courtly perfection.

It is known that Castiglione's *Book of the Courtier* played an important role in the propagation of this myth.[10] Again, the influence of the book can be gauged by the endorsement it received (sometimes in the form of borrowing) from moralists who *complain* about courtly misdemeanor. Until the 1590s anti-courtly critics did not challenge Castiglione's prescriptions as much as they referred to them as desirable norms. In *The Scholemaster* (published posthumously in 1570) Roger Ascham makes one of the sternest attacks on court conduct and Italianate manners to be found in the period. For instance, he condemns the courtly conception of grace in these words:

> For, if a yong ientleman, be demeure, and still of nature, they say, he is simple and lacketh witte. . . . If he be innocent and ignorant of ill, they say, he is rude, and hath no grace, so ungraciouslie do som gracelesse men, misuse the faire and godlie word GRACE. But if ye

[9] William Harrison, *The Description of England*, ed. Georges Edelen (Ithaca, N.Y., 1968), pp. 229-230.

[10] For studies of *The Courtier*'s influence in Elizabethan England see Introduction, note 1.

would know, what grace they meene, go, and looke, and
learne emonges them, and ye shall see that it is: First, to
blush at nothing . . . then foloweth, to dare do any mis-
chief, to contemne stoutly any goodnesse, to be busie in
every matter, to be skilfull in every thing, to acknowledge
no ignorance at all. To do thus in Court, is counted of
some the chief and greatest grace of all: and termed by
the name of a vertue. . . . Moreover, where the swing
goeth, there to follow, fawn, flatter, laugh and lie lustelie
at other mens liking. . . .[11]

In the relative absence of complaints against Elizabeth's
court Ascham's stands out as a bold denunciation of cur-
rent fashion. But even this lone critic qualifies his attack.
Despite his anti-Italian bias and his contempt for courtly
sophistications, he endorses Castiglione's book and acknowl-
edges its positive value: "To ioyne learnyng with cumlie
exercises, *Conto Baldesar Castiglione* in his booke, *Cortegi-
ano* doth trimlie teache: which booke advisedlie read, and
diligentlie folowed, but one year at home in England, would
do a yong ientleman more good, I wisse, then three yeares
travell abrode spent in Italie."[12] He then goes on to promote
Hoby's translation, which had recently appeared in 1561.
Ascham does not seem disturbed by the contradiction
emerging from his approval of Castiglione's handbook and
his condemnation of courtly grace. He must have known
how often the notion of grace is extolled in the *Cortegiano*,
and how vulnerable that notion could be when put into
practice. "To blush at nothing . . . to be skilfull in every
thyng, to acknowledge no ignorance at all," are manners
disturbingly close to those advocated in the Italian book.
Yet no relation is made between the degeneration he con-
demns and what the book prescribes. Obviously he believes
that the prescriptions can and will be "diligentlie folowed"
without becoming the misconduct he condemns. To further

[11] Roger Ascham, *English Works*, ed. W. A. Wright (Cambridge,
1904), pp. 206-207.
[12] *Ibid.*, p. 218.

attest his faith in courtiership, he recommends imitating the model behavior of the queen, flatteringly depicted as the perfect courtier.

Ascham's criticism of the court's manners qualified by his faith in its possibilities of model conduct is a recurrent feature of Elizabethan anti-courtly sentiment for nearly two decades after the publication of *The Scholemaster*. It can be found, for example, in Spenser's *Mother Hubberds Tale*. Though this complaint was published in revised form only in 1591, Spenser states in the dedication to Lady Compton that the poem was "long sithens composed in the raw conceipt of my youth," and it has been argued that the bulk of it may have been written as early as 1579-1580.[13] In the guise of an animal fable the *Tale* bitterly exposes at one stage the corruptions of court life. Spenser aims his attack at individuals, represented by the Fox and the Ape of the fable, who abuse and debase the laws of courtesy. Through their actions he also reveals the success of imposture at court as well as the vices it tolerates. Yet despite his satirical indictment he does not forsake the myth of the perfect courtier. While describing the aberrations of the Fox and the Ape, the poet gives us a detailed portrait of the "rightful Courtier" (lines 717-793) that is virtually a poetic summary of the *Cortegiano*, though Spenser emphasizes more than did Castiglione the courtier's civic and political attributes. Serving as a foil to the vicious conduct he satirizes, this portrayal attests his faith in the possibility of model courtliness. Again, as with Ascham, Spenser's contempt for abject courtiers could not extend to the total rejection of a social system which tolerated their abuses, particularly since

[13] Reasons for dating the original version of *Mother Hubberds Tale* as early as 1579-1580 were put forth by Edwin Greenlaw in "Spenser and the Earl of Leicester," *PMLA* 25 (1910), 535-561. A. C. Judson concurs with this dating of the poem in his *Life of Edmund Spenser* (Baltimore, 1945), pp. 68-71, 153-155; and in a later note, "Mother Hubberds' Ape," *MLN* 63 (1948), 145-149, Judson remarks that although the evidence for the early dating is not conclusive, Greenlaw's thesis has not been refuted.

some commitment to the system was necessary for his pro-
fessional survival. I will soon argue that Spenser's anti-
courtly attitudes become less qualified later in his career. But
in this earlier poem his indignation remains partial: his
portrait of a corrupt court is balanced by the vision, em-
bodied in the description of the "brave courtier," of its
regeneration.

If patriotism and the necessities of homage to their queen
were some of the reasons why late Tudor moralists praised
"the better race in Court" (the phrase is Ben Jonson's)
while deploring the corruptions of the institution, for a good
part of Elizabeth's reign they also genuinely believed that
under her influence the court had become the nation's cen-
ter of moral and cultural authority. Such faith in the sov-
ereign and her chief courtiers balanced, even at times out-
weighed, their recognition of the court's abuses. To some
extent the belief in model courtiership was strengthened
by actual example. Aside from Puttenham's testimony there
is evidence, we saw earlier, that Elizabeth and her leading
courtiers achieved the kind of beautiful conduct Castiglione
had prescribed. Sir Philip Sidney, for one, was thought by
his contemporaries to have embodied some of the perfec-
tion envisaged in *The Courtier*. Thomas Nashe explicitly
associates the book and the man in one of the ʹmany praises
bestowed on Sidney after his early death:

> So it was, that not long since lighting in company with
> manie extraordinarie Gentlemen, of most excellent parts,
> it was my chance . . . to moove divers Questions, as touch-
> ing the severall qualities required in *Castalions* Courtier:
> one came in with that of *Ovid, Semper amabilis esto*,
> another stood more stricktly on the necessitie of that
> affabilitie, which our Latinists entitle *facetus*, & we more
> familiarlie describe by the name of discoursing: the third
> came in with his carpet devises and tolde what it was to
> tickle a Citterne, or have a sweete stroke on the Lute, to
> daunce more delicatlie, and revell it bravelie. The fourth
> as an enemie to their faction, confuted all these as effem-

inate follies, and woulde needes maintaine, that the onely adjuncts of a Courtier were schollership and courage. . . . This discourse thus continued . . . but this was the upshot, that England afforded many mediocrities, but never saw any thing more singuler than worthy Sir *Phillip Sidney*, of whom it might truely be saide, *Arma virumque cano*.[14]

Obviously the myth of the perfect courtier was not just kept alive by Sidney's example, but it is hardly coincidental that a few years after his death in 1586 one notes, in the literature, a marked decline in the belief that courtiers could live up to the model roles Castiglione and others had imagined. During the decade that follows the publication of Puttenham's *Arte* in 1589, though English writers continue to express faith in the amending powers of their sovereign, they become increasingly skeptical of the establishment she governs. Her court seems to lose the respect and admiration it previously enjoyed. Why did this change occur?

The generational turnover that took place at court around 1590 provides part of the answer. Soon after Sidney's premature death many of the leading courtiers of Elizabeth's generation also died: the Earl of Leicester in 1588; Sir Walter Mildmay, one the queen's oldest ministers, in 1589; Blanche Parry, chief gentlewoman of the Privy Chamber, the Earl of Warwick, and Sir Francis Walsingham, all in

[14] *The Anatomie of Absurditie* (1589) in *The Works of Thomas Nashe*, ed. R. B. McKerrow (London, 1966), I, 7. Though the legend of Sir Philip as the perfect Renaissance courtier really grows after his early death in 1586, already in a letter of March 25, 1578, we find his father telling Robert Sidney to imitate his older brother Philip's "Vertues, Exercyses, Studyes, and Accyons: he ys a rare Ornament of thys Age, the very Formular, that all well dysposed young Gentylmen of ouer Court, do form allsoe thear Maners and Lyfe by." *Letters and Memorials of State in the Reigns of Queen Mary, Queen Elizabeth, King James, . . .* ed. Arthur Collins (London, 1746), I, 246. Richard Lanham has persuasively argued that the Sidney legend is not at all points supported by fact and that, in many ways, it is an extension of the Elizabethan myth of the perfect courtier. See his "Sidney: The Ornament of his Age," *Southern Review* 2 (1967), 319-340.

1590; Sir Christopher Hatton in 1591. Burghley continued
to grow old with his queen (he died in 1598), but both his
dominance as her chief minister of patronage and his sta-
bilizing influence in that role on the destructive competition
for royal favor were waning. The disappearance of Lei-
cester, Walsingham, and Hatton intensified that competition
as a new generation of courtiers aspired to fill the vacuum
they had left. Chief among this new group of courtiers were
the young Earl of Essex, Sir Walter Ralegh, and Burghley's
son, Robert Cecil. In the course of their struggle for power
the tone and conduct of court politics underwent a dis-
cernible change. First of all, their rise, especially that of
Essex, disrupted the balance of power among the court's
factions so carefully forged earlier in the reign. The his-
torian Sir John Neale comments on this change in a well-
known article on the Elizabethan political scene:

> In the first decade of Elizabeth's reign there were occa-
> sions when faction seemed to be getting of hand. But there
> was then a fundamental harmony in age and outlook
> between sovereign and statesmen. Leicester was not an
> Essex, and the loyalty, authority, and uprightness of such
> men as William Cecil, Nicholas Bacon, and the Earl of
> Bedford, to mention no others, were sufficient steadying
> force. Sir Robert Naunton, in his *Fragmenta Regalia*, has
> an astute comment on the Queen's method of govern-
> ment. "The principal note of her reign will be, that she
> ruled much by faction and parties, which herself both
> made, upheld, and weakened, as her own great judgment
> advised." As Sir Henry Wotton wrote, it "was not the
> least ground of much of her quiet and success."
>
> The 1590s, however, were a political climacteric. The
> great statesmen and faction-leaders of the reign were
> passing in rapid succession to the grave; and power had
> to be transferred to the new generation at a pace dan-
> gerous to the digestive capacity of the system. The "quiet
> and success" which Elizabeth had derived from the rivalry
> of the factions were shattered, principally by the nature

of the young Earl of Essex, but also by the survival of Burghley, whose unrivalled experience, authority, and subtlety were all concentrated on securing the succession to his very able son, Robert Cecil.[15]

In his article Neale also draws attention to another, more pertinent change in court life during the last decade of the reign: corruption began to afflict the queen's court much more severely than it had previously, and standards of official morality deteriorated markedly. The evidence also suggests that the new generation of courtiers exercised their power and office with less probity than the preceding one. Neither corruption nor intense rivalry, Neale remarks, could be avoided in a system of personal monarchy with immense patronage at the disposal of the Crown, and inadequate salaries in both royal and private households.[16] But in the 1590s, as he points out, there were other distinct economic and social causes responsible for the marked downward trend in the court's public morality:

> The growing wealth of the nation, in contrast with that of the state; monetary inflation; industrial expansion, coupled with the scandal of monopolies; perhaps, also, an undue concentration of money on the domestic market owing to war conditions: all these probably help to explain soaring bribes and the feverish competition for place and favour. It has the appearance of an inflationary movement: too many suitors pursuing too few privileges. Nor must we forget that the Queen was ageing, and her discipline—dependent in any case upon the loyalty and

[15] J. E. Neale, "The Elizabethan Political Scene," (British Academy Raleigh Lecture, 1948), reprinted in *Essays in Elizabethan History* (London, 1958), pp. 79-80.

[16] For more detailed accounts than Neale's of the offices, favors, and general patronage at Elizabeth's disposal and which drew the nobility to her court, see W. T. MacCaffrey, "Place and Patronage in Elizabethan Politics," *Elizabethan Government and Society*, ed. S. T. Bindoff, J. Hurstfield, and C. H. Williams (London, 1961), pp. 99-108; and Lawrence Stone, *The Crisis of the Aristocracy 1558-1641* (Oxford, 1965), "Office and the Court," pp. 385-504.

probity of those about her—losing its old resilience. . . .

In leaving this tale of growing corruption, we may reflect . . . that a new generation does not respond so readily to the restraints of a moral code which it inherits and does not create. The generation coming into power in the 1590s was out of tune with the old Queen and her ways. It fawned but it deceived. Elizabeth herself voiced this feeling to her faithful antiquary, William Lambarde, in 1601: "Now the wit of the fox is everywhere on foot, so as hardly a faithful or virtuous man may be found."[17]

Neale's account of the growing corruption and decay in government during the last decade of Elizabeth's reign has been substantiated by other historians. "His [Neale's] contention," writes Lawrence Stone, "that the 1590s saw a positive deterioration in official morality is supported by the lack of offers of bribes in ealier petitions to the Cecils. It is possible, even likely that Leicester had been very corrupt, but all the evidence suggests that it was not till the 1590s that venality became widespread. And it is the spread which is important. . . ." Stone points out that it had always been an acceptable practice to give court officials various gifts—like delicacies, a falcon, or a horse—to sweeten the course of petitions and offers. Also acceptable were well-established fees that every official exacted 'from the public for executing his duties. What became particularly abused, however, was the system of "gratuities" whereby courtiers were paid for particular services rendered,

> whether it be the grant of an office or a patent of monopoly, a pardon for a murderer or a license to export beer. . . . all these things and many more were at the disposal of the monarch, and between her and the suitor there was massed a tight phalanx of courtiers. Access was impossible without a friend at Court, and that friendship was up for sale.[18]

[17] "The Elizabethan Political Scene," pp. 78-79.
[18] *The Crisis of the Aristocracy 1558-1641* (Oxford, 1965), pp. 490, 491. For further comments on the decay of court prestige in the

Among the factors that "accelerated the drift up to and beyond the acceptable threshold of corruption" Stone emphasizes the impoverishment of the court aristocracy, faced in a time of inflation with the increasing financial burden of court and office. Had Elizabeth been more willing to relieve that burden, her officials would have had less reason to resort to bribery to maintain themselves. But "in the 1580's and 1590's," Stone explains, "the appalling cost of the Anglo-Spanish War, coupled with a natural parsimony which increased with old age, induced Queen Elizabeth severely to reduce her gifts to all except her favourite, the Earl of Essex—and even he was hard put to it to make ends meet."[19]

External factors such as the queen's parsimony or the temptations of war finance were not solely responsible for spreading corruption at court. Corruption was also the result, as Stone puts it, of "a distinct weakening of moral integrity on the part of the rising generation of courtiers."

> The level to which public morality had sunk when Elizabeth died is perhaps best illustrated by a letter of Sir Robert Cecil to his secretary Michael Hicks, written in February 1604. He is trying to obtain a favor for his protégé, Fulke Greville, but explains that it is necessary to obtain Lord Buckhurst's support. He therefore instructs Hicks to offer Lady Glemham £100 to give to her father, adding the warning not to hand over the cash in advance "or else she may cosin you." Finally he adds a postscript: "For ye 100[li] I will find a ward to pay it."

1590s see also Lawrence Stone, *The Causes of the English Revolution 1529-1642* (London, 1972), pp. 79-91. In this later study Stone observes that "There had inevitably been a great deal of corruption [at the highest level of government] during the hectic years of seizure of Church property and its disposal on the market between 1536 and 1551, but the more efficient administrators, such as Sir William Cecil, had slowly reimposed some sense of order and responsibility. *The levels both of corruption and of protest against it seems to have subsided between about 1552 and 1588*" (p. 86, italics mine).

[19] *The Crisis of the Aristocracy*, pp. 488-489.

Here is a letter written by a Secretary of State and Master of the Court of Wards about a Lord Treasurer. It takes for granted that the latter's support can be bought, and offers to find the money for the bribe by a corrupt use of official authority. Such was the condition to which Elizabeth's parsimony and their own defects of character had reduced the great officials and court peers.[20]

Although the rotting political situation in the 1590s anticipates what is to come under the rule of James I, one must be careful not to attribute to Elizabeth's court characteristics that belong to the Jacobean one. Venality did spread in her court in the last decade of her reign, but it was not yet as universal as it became under the early Stuarts. Elizabeth's discipline may have waned in her last years, but she still exerted control and did not give rein to the forces of corruption. Moreover, her own probity counterbalanced the abuses perpetrated by some of her servants. "Under Elizabeth," Stone remarks, "government spokesmen could at least ask the Commons to grant taxes with a clear conscience. 'Where,' asked Bacon in 1592, 'be the wasteful buildings and the exorbitant and prodigal donatives, the sumptuous dissipations in pleasures and vain ostentations, which we find have exhausted the coffers of so many kings?' Where indeed, if we ignore the grants to Leicester and Essex? But no such defence could be put up for King James."[21] While the courtiers' financial exploitation of their position as intermediaries between the sovereign and her subjects served to lessen the latter's respect for the court, the queen herself continued to win her countrymen's loyalty and reverence. Still, there can be no doubt that the marked deterioration of the court's public morality in the 1590s was responsible for the growing disenchantment Elizabethans began showing toward the queen's establishment and its members. There were, to be sure, other long-term factors at work that were undermining the courtier's privileged status: for example, changes in the techniques of

[20] *Ibid.*, p. 492.   [21] *Ibid.*, p. 495.

warfare that reduced the military role of the court aristocracy; the growth of bureaucratic professionalization and the government's increasing reliance on career administrators; the widening gap between the ethical standards and way of life of the court and those of the country; and, of course, the rise of puritanism. Yet none of these causes for the gradual erosion of the courtier's social, moral, and political authority seems as prominent and discernible in the 1590s as the rapid downward trend in the court's official conduct.

Symptoms of the consequent loss of faith in the myth of the perfect courtier are equally discernible. *The Book of the Courtier*, for example, loses its prominence as a code of behavior. It continues to be read and to be admired. But already at the end of Elizabeth's reign its authority is challenged by new courtesy books, devoted to fashioning polite gentlemen acting in society at large rather than courtiers. In *The Courtier*'s most notable rival, Stefano Guazzo's *Civile Conversation* (translated into English as early as 1581), the civil and honest behavior recommended often defies courtly notions of politeness. The anti-courtly bias in Guazzo's handbook, its open criticism of dissimulation, ornamentation, and dilettantism, stem from the author's awareness that many of the beautiful tactics recommended in court conduct were all too prone, in actual practice, to lapse into shallowness and fraud.[22] So the declining influence of *The Courtier* can partly be attributed to the fact that a growing number of Englishmen came to share Guazzo's perception that Castiglione's norms of politeness could not but be abused in the vicious struggle for favor at court. By

---

[22] For a fuller discussion of the differences between courtly norms of politeness and those advocated in *The Civile Conversation* see my article, "Rival Arts of Conduct in Elizabethan England: Guazzo's *Civile Conversation* and Castiglione's *Courtier*," *Yearbook of Italian Studies* 1 (1971), 178-198; the popularity Guazzo's conduct book already enjoyed by the end of Elizabeth's reign is well-documented in John L. Lievsay, *Stefano Guazzo and the English Renaissance 1575-1675* (Chapel Hill, 1961).

the 1590s, Elizabethan moralists who condemn the court's vices no longer pay homage to exemplary courtliness or Castiglione's book, as they did before, to offset their condemnation. So little faith seems to remain in the possibility of model comportment at court that the abuses deplored there come to be regarded as the normal features of courtliness rather than its aberrations. The distinction made earlier between proper court conduct and its degenerate forms seems to collapse. At any rate, anti-courtly writers cease to acknowledge such a distinction. For example, in the satires that flourished at the end of the 1590s, the animus against the uses and abuses of Castiglione's code becomes so marked that the affected fop ridiculed in these works is occasionally referred to as "a Castilio."[23] In general, the satires of John Donne, Edward Guilpin, Joseph Hall, John Marston—a new generation of writers—usher in much more uncompromising anti-courtly attitudes, which only intensify with the coming of James I to the throne. But even the older generation of authors who previously espoused the myth of the perfect courtier tend to forsake it in the 1590s.

Spenser shows an increasing disaffection with courtly behavior in the work that follows the publication of the first three books of *The Faerie Queene* in 1590. His shift of attitude becomes noticeable in *Colin Clouts Come Home Againe*, first published in 1595 but dedicated to Ralegh in 1591. Set in an Irish pastoral setting, the poem consists in large part of the shepherd Colin Clout's account (one that bears close resemblance to Spenser's own experience) of his visit to the Queen's court and his eventual return to the more appealing rustic life he had left behind. Even a brief

[23] For Marston's use of "Castilio" or "Absolute Castilio" as a pejorative term describing the courtly fop see his *Certaine Satyres* (1598), Satire 1, and *The Scourge of Villanie* (1598), "In Lectores prorsus indignos," in *The Poems of John Marston*, ed. Arnold Davenport (Liverpool, 1961), pp. 68, 96. One reason the satirists refer to Castiglione as Castilio may stem from the fact that Thomas Hoby, his first English translator, referred to him by that name. The original title of Hoby's translation in 1561 was *The Courtyer of Count Baldessar Castilio*.

look at it reveals that its author could no longer sustain his earlier belief in courtly perfection. Spenser's view of the court does remain ambivalent throughout the poem, yet the anti-courtly sentiments expressed in it are no longer offset, as they were in *Mother Hubberds Tale*, by a faith in the exemplary conduct of "right" courtiers. Now it seems that the anti-courtliness is chiefly balanced by a faith in the virtuous power of one individual—Queen Elizabeth. And while the poem celebrates the civilized sophistication of her court, it also deplores the corrupt manners such sophistication breeds. Even Colin's elaborate praises of the queen's establishment cannot end without serious qualifications. No sooner has he offered his bumptious fellow shepherds a dazzling description of the court as a place where "learned arts do flourish in great honor / And Poets wits are had in peerlesse price" (320-321), than he has to add:

　all good, all grace there freely growes,
Had people grace it gratefully to use:
For God his gifts there plenteously bestowes,
But gracelesse men them greatly do abuse (324-328).[24]

Later, in his splendid praises of Elizabeth (595-615), which follow his tribute to the ladies of the court, Colin conveys his sense of awe at the splendor and magnificence surrounding the queen. But admiration and bedazzlement are sharply undercut when he shifts from praising his sovereign to denouncing the fraud and duplicity plaguing the establishment she governs. "For sooth to say," warns Colin,

　　it is no sort of life,
For shepheard fit to lead in that same place,
Where each one seeks with malice and with strife,
To thrust downe other into foule disgrace,

[24] Quotations of *Colin Clouts Come Home Againe* are taken from *The Works of Edmund Spenser. A Variorum Edition*, ed. Edwin Greenlaw, Charles G. Osgood, et al. (Baltimore, 1932-1957), *The Minor Poems* I, 147-172. Hereafter all citations of Spenser's poetry come from this edition, which I will refer to as: Spenser, *Works*, Variorum Edition.

Himselfe to raise: and he doth soonest rise
That best can handle his deceitfull wit,
In subtil shifts, and finest sleights devise,
Either by slaundring his well deemed name,
Through leasings lewd, and feigned forgerie:
Or else by breeding him some blot of blame,
By creeping close into his secrecie;
To which him needs, a guilefull hollow hart,
Masked with faire dissembling curtesie,
A filed toung furnisht with tearmes of art,
No art of schoole, but Courtiers schoolery (688-702).

Although the court's deceitful ways were always a tradi-
tional target of satirical complaint, it is unusual to find them
denounced so obsessively, even by others who had sued at
court in vain. And no longer does the author propose that
the deceit and the "vaunted vanitie" he also decries (711-
730) are deviations from model norms of conduct. When
immediately after this indictment of the court's corrupt
ways Hobbinol complains,

Ah Colin . . . the blame
Which thou imputest, is too generall,
As if not any gentle wit of name,
Nor honest mynd might there be found at all (731-734),

Colin's retraction is hardly optimistic. He admits that "full
many persons of right worthie parts" can still be found in
the court, but he gives no indication that their virtues suf-
fice to redeem the court's vices. True, Colin does not lose
faith in the amending powers of Elizabeth. But she be-
comes in the poem (as elsewhere in Spenser's later poetry)
increasingly distinct from the court she dominates. This
discrepancy between his criticism of the court and the
praise of its ruler may be forced upon the poet by the
exigencies of patronage. But it is also Spenser's way of con-
veying the contradictory sense of political loyalty and
moral dismay he feels towards the royal establishment.
Moreover, by tying together his praise of the court's mag-

tinguish from the artist who fashioned him. At least twice, in fact, he is referred to as a "maker" (I. i. 45 and 46), and were it not for the dire effects of his magic, were the sources of his power not shown to be diabolical, Archimago could be taken for a figure of the poet rather than the nightmare version of one he represents. Spenser tells us from the start that his art, unlike Archimago's, is divinely inspired. But in the course of beguiling us with "true-seeming lyes," he remains all too aware of the thin line that separates his fiction from the malice of its evil enchanters. Actually, in some of the Proems, which preface each book of the epic, the author intimates that some contemporaries will fail to distinguish his fiction from the fraud and deceit he condemns. For example, in the Proem to Book II Spenser anticipates "That all this famous antique history / Of some the aboundance of an idle braine / Will judged be, and painted forgery." He defends himself against such charges by alerting his readers to the important truths veiled beneath the surface of his romance. But even so, he feels uneasy enough about his allegorical dissimulations to explain apologetically to his sovereign what his motives are for representing her and her realm so covertly (II. Pr. 5). To ward off accusations that he too practices false-seeming, Spenser has to take pains to distinguish evil duplicity from his legitimate use of "fayned colors shading a true case" (V. vii. 2). This effort is reflected in the particular indignation he shows towards a Duessa and the numerous other agents in the poem who perpetrate "fraud or fayned blandishment." He reserves his greatest moral outrage for these characters precisely because they violate the processes on which his poetry as well as all civilized intercourse depend.

It should be said that in *The Faerie Queene* the author does not specifically define fraud and duplicity as courtly vices but shows them to plague society in general. A basic premise governing the pattern of Spenser's epic makes it difficult for him to express the anti-courtly sentiments evident in some of his minor poems. All the virtuous exploits in the work originate in Gloriana's court, the matrix of the poem's imagined world. The author began by assuming that Elizabeth's court like Gloriana's Court in the fiction, could fulfill exemplary moral and social functions in the society it dominated. Despite his having lost faith in the court's role as "the great schoolmistresse of Courtesy," despite his scorn for the "Courtiers schoolery" it actually bred, he could not abandon the idea that the court had to remain a center of moral as well as political governance without jeopardizing both the unity of his poem and its didactic intent. Nevertheless, in the second installment of the epic (Books IV-VI, published in 1596), it becomes more difficult for the author to suppress his disenchantment with the court. Increasingly he refers to the art of false-seeming as a courtly vocation. For the most part these anti-courtly remarks are made in passing, but made repeatedly enough to indicate that the dissociation Spenser wishes to assert between his artistic feigning and malevolent deceit cannot but entail a dissociation of his poetic practices from those of the courtier.[26]

The anti-courtliness that marks Spenser's later work indicates how impossible it became in the 1590s for poets to invoke courtly manners in support of their art. Previously when these manners had reached a level of refinement surpassing that of early Elizabethan poetry, it made sense for Puttenham to prescribe them as a model of style. And when the court's conduct won the admiration of Englishmen, the art of poets could gain equal respect by having affinities with it. However, Elizabethan poets rapidly achieved a stylistic mastery even greater than Puttenham had anticipated. Simultaneously the court began losing her authority as "the great schoolmistress of courtesy." Poetry could no longer profit from being identified with court conduct. Poets did not come to feel so secure that they could forego

[26] I am thinking of passages like: "guyle and malice and despight / That under shew oftimes of fayned semblance / Are wont in Princes court to work great scath" (F.Q. v. ix. 22); or "Therein he them full faire did entertaine / Not with such forged showes, as fitter beene / For courting fooles, that curtesies would faine, / But with entire affection and appearaunce plaine" (F.Q. vi. v. 38).

the supporting example of civilized manners. But courtliness, instead of being admired for the cultivation of such manners, became increasingly criticized for its corruption of them. Beautiful court style, when not judiciously exercised, risked lapsing into the worst abuses. It wasn't simply that the risk became a reality. Some immoral or ridiculous behavior could always be found at Elizabeth's as at any royal court. But as long as "the better race in Court" won respect and admiration for its comportment, the inevitable abuses of courtliness were deplored as such. However, when official court conduct so deteriorated—as it seems to have done in the 1590s—that the respect for, and the belief in, model courtliness could no longer be sustained, then gradually the abuses came to be regarded as normal features of court conduct rather than as aberrations. When behavior at court became equated with excessive artificiality, deceit, fraud, and frivolity, the poet or his supporters could hardly turn to its practice to justify his use of ornament, his dissimulation, or his playfulness. The poet could afford even less to have his art associated with courtliness, since his deceptions, though delightful and benevolent, risked being identified with the malicious lying and deceit that courtiers were now regularly seen to practice.

However, when no longer shadowed by the model example of courtly conduct, poets began to assert their own mastery of beautiful manners. For having perfected rather than abused their art, they still displayed the beautiful manners that courtiers now more often violated. As a result of the declining respect for the art of courtiership the art of poetry gradually assumed its model role. Already in the *Apology for Poetry* Sidney had intimated that the civilizing influence ideally expected of courtiers behaving in poetic ways had to be confined to the possibilities of poetry itself. By 1595, when his defense of poetry was posthumously published, that intimation seemed fully confirmed. Courtiers had proven incapable of living up to the model role expected of them. Yet the esthetic and moral functions that had been ascribed to them could still be fulfilled by the poet, the one agent who so resembled the courtier. The analogies, for instance, between the stylistic aspects of poetry and courtliness disclosed in *The Arte of English Poesie* still applied, even though courtiers abused rather than exercised the rules of beautiful conduct. Puttenham had assumed that the poet could perfect his verbal conduct by imitating the manners of the courtier. But when the faith in exemplary courtliness disappears, not even a decade after the *Arte* is published, the assumption could be reversed. In the absence of any courtly models of comportment, the poet's special attributes qualify *him* as the maker of manners, and he emerges as the one who can impart lessons of conduct to the courtier.

This idea that the courtier must turn to the poet to learn proper courtesy can be found subtly expressed in Spenser's sixth book of *The Faerie Queene*. It had to be expressed subtly. The deterioration of court conduct notwithstanding, the aristocracy still considered the setting of society's standards of politeness its rightful prerogative. It would be presumptuous, not to say perilous, for the poet to maintain openly that his social betters (who made up a large part of the audience) had forfeited this prerogative and, hence, compelled him to assume it. For Spenser to assert this new jurisdiction was all the more difficult because of his dependence on royal favor. Yet with remarkable tact he does propose in Book vi that the teaching of courtesy has become the poet's responsibility. The claim is facilitated by the fact that he redefines courtesy as a basically internal virtue and thereby distinguishes it from courtly politeness, of which the attributes are largely external. One can understand from his growing reservations about rhetoric, external gestures, and, in general, "the outward shew of things that only seem" why he would emphasize the internal sources of courtesy.[27] Neither is it surprising that in the course of establishing the poet's role as a maker of manners in Book

[27] The best general consideration of Spenser's misgivings about pageant, language, and men's outward shows in *The Faerie Queene* is to be found in A. Bartlett Giamatti's *Play of Double Senses: Spenser's Faerie Queene* (Englewood Cliffs, N.J., 1975), esp. Chs. viii, x, and xi. I am indebted to this recent study.

VI Spenser will not emphasize his stylistic attributes but dwell on his unique inner gifts: poetic inspiration and the privileged vision that comes with it. He had expressed too many previous doubts in his epic about men's manipulations of their exterior selves and of their speech to propose that the poet's jurisdiction resided in his ability to manipulate language, however beautifully he did it. I suggested earlier that his actual misgivings about the correlation Puttenham could draw between poetry and courtliness had prompted him to insist on the difference between the poet and the various sinister agents in *The Faerie Queene* so "cunningly able to dissemble." Even if he recognized that Puttenham's correlation was now reversed, namely that the courtier could perfect his manners by emulating the poet's verbal graces, he could not, in good conscience, make a case of it. Spenser will not, however, totally disregard the stylistic virtues that also warrant the poet's authority as a maker of manners. The very subtlety with which Book VI affirms the latter's new social importance proves how adept the poet really is at being cunning and indirect—so adept, in fact, that the courtier-reader can only learn from his example. But this is to anticipate a discussion that requires another and final chapter.

Chapter V

Spenser's moral design in each book of *The Faerie Queene* was to define a particular virtue by allegorical means and instill it in the minds of the aristocratic readers he particularly sought to address. The purpose of the entire epic, he had claimed at the start, was "to fashion a gentleman or noble person in vertuous and gentle discipline." Given that epic poets had been acknowledged as moral and civic teachers ever since antiquity, and that their poems were assumed to offer readers models of virtue, Spenser's didactic motives seem quite traditional. Nor does it seem very surprising that "a gentleman or noble person" might require fashioning in holiness, temperance, chastity, or the other virtues mirrored in the books preceding Book VI, "The Legend of Courtesie." But in the context of my previous discussion, it does seem striking that Spenser should choose to lecture his social superiors on their courtesy. One would assume that such readers, given their birth and upbringing, were already adept enough in matters of polite intercourse not to require further lessons in good manners. Besides, if Elizabethan courtiers were still considered, as they had been, society's arbiters of politeness there would seem to be even less reason for teaching them courtesy. By announcing that this virtue will be the subject of Book VI, Spenser immediately challenges such assumptions. His decision to mirror the virtue suggests that either his aristocratic readers actually lack true politeness or else that courtesy consists of more than a mastery of social etiquette. To be sure, the writing of any Renaissance "mirror" or conduct book constituted an act of social criticism, since the point of composing such a work was to *improve* the actual conduct of those it addressed. Still, when one considers the authority Elizabethan aristocrats were accorded as makers of manners, Spenser's intent to fashion them in courtesy seems particularly defiant. Why would he feel obliged to define proper courtesy in his epic unless he felt that it was no longer practiced or possessed by those supposedly courteous? The very title of his last finished book implies that he has lost

faith in the court's preeminence as "the schoolmistress of
courtesy." It also indicates that he, as a poet, has now ap-
propriated the role of shaping his nation's beautiful manners.
But before the reader has time to consider the new social
assumptions implicit in the Sixth Book's title, Spenser in-
forms him in the Proem why he feels called upon to restore
courtesy to its proper form.

Courtesy, Spenser maintains in the invocation that begins
the Proem, now lies hidden from men's eyes and can only
be apprehended by poetic inspiration, which he calls upon
the Muses to grant him:

> Ye sacred imps that on *Parnasso* dwell,
> And there the keeping haue of learnings threasures,
> Which doe all wordly riches farre excell,
>
> .   .   .   .
>
> Guyde ye my footing, and conduct me well
> In these strange waies, where neuer foote did use,
> Ne none can find, but who was taught them by the Muse.
>
> Reuele to me the sacred noursery
> Of vertue, which with you doth there remaine,
> Where it in silver bowre does hidden ly
> From view of men, and wicked worlds disdaine.
>
> .   .   .   .
>
> Amongst them all growes not a fayrer flowre,
> Then is the bloosme of comely courtesie,
> Which though it on a lowly stalke doe bowre,
> Yet brancheth forth in braue nobilitie,
> And spreds it selfe through all ciuilitie:
> Of which though present age does plenteous seeme,
> Yet being matcht with plaine Antiquitie,
> Ye will them all but fayned showes esteeme,
> Which carry colours faire, that feeble eies misdeeme.
>
> But in the triall of true curtesie,
> Its now so farre from that, which then it was,
> That it indeed is nought but forgerie,
> Fashion'd to please the eies of them, that pas,
> Which see not perfect things but in a glas:

Yet is that glasse so gay, that it can blynd
The wisest sight, to thinke gold that is bras.
But vertues seat is deepe within the mynd,
And not in outward shows, but inward thoughts defynd.

(VI. Pr. 2-5)[1]

Not only does Spenser use the conventions of epic invocation to make a bold claim about the special privilege of poetic insight, he evokes in these lines the social conditions that justify his claim. Ostensibly, he contrasts the semblance of courtesy in the present age with its ideal pattern, in "plaine Antiquitie," a form that now only the poet, by force of imaginative insight, is allowed to see and recreate. But the difference between courtesy "as it is" and "as it was," expressed here in temporal dimensions of epic size, can also be reduced to the poet's own experience of change. His nostalgia for a virtuous if fictive past is conditioned to some extent by the memory of his belief in courtly perfection, now dispelled by present doubts. Though his complaints about modern courtesy remain generalized, he implies that the court's abdication of its exemplary role prompts his mission to restore a lost ideal of the virtue. "Fayned showes" and "forgerie," the terms in which he describes courtesy's present decay, recall his use of "fained forgerie" and "faire dissembling curtesie" to define "Courtiers schoolery" in *Colin Clouts Come Home Againe*. Yet just as in the earlier poem Colin's criticism of the court was qualified by his eulogy of the queen, so in this proem the condemnation levelled at courtly manners is balanced by praise of Elizabeth's virtue. Spenser may enhance "antique courtesy" by contrasting it with its corrupt present state, but he reserves the utmost compliment for his sovereign:

But where shall I in all Antiquity
So faire a patterne finde, where may be seene
The goodly praise of Princely curtesie,
As in your selfe, O soveraine Lady Queene,

[1] As before, my quotations of Spenser's poetry are taken from the *Works*, Variorum Edition.

In whose pure minde, as in a mirrour sheene,
It showes, and with her brightnesse doth inflame
The eyes of all, which thereon fixed beene;

. . . .

Then pardon me, most dreaded Soveraine,
That from your selfe I doe this vertue bring,
And to your selfe doe it returne againe:
So from the Ocean all riuers spring,
And tribute backe repay as to their King.
Right so from you all goodly vertues well
Into the rest, which round about you ring,
Faire Lords and Ladies, which about you dwell,
And doe adorne your Court, were courtesies excell.

(VI. Pr. 6-7)

How can one reconcile the discrepancy between the poet's censure of his age and his lavish praise of the queen who dominates that age? The final lines of the Proem, which eulogize the court's "Faire Lords and Ladies," seem particularly contradictory after the thinly veiled anti-courtliness expressed in the earlier stanzas. Again, it seems, Spenser is reluctant to abandon hope in the court's exemplary possibilities even while he suggests that courtesy has fled from it. His flattery attests his continuing belief that those at the center of power can still fulfill the ideals his art calls upon them to emulate. Yet the poet's praise serves more than the traditional function of presenting ideal images to which the governing class may ascend. So the contradictions in the Proem reflect more than another instance of the qualified anti-courtliness Spenser displays throughout his poetry. Until the Proem praises the queen as the paragon of courtesy, it proclaims that the poet alone can project the pattern of courtesy men must emulate. It proposes that the poet, by virtue of his unique talents, has become most qualified to serve as his nation's maker of manners. As much as Spenser has come to believe this, the exigencies of patronage and decorum compel him to acknowledge that the queen remains the inspiring model of all virtuous conduct. His very need

with the social threats besetting the world. Calidore's inade-
quacy is conveyed largely by his inability to overcome the
Blatant Beast, that enigmatic symbol of uncivility ravaging
the social order of Spenser's fiction. The hero leaves the
narrative in the third canto pursuing the Beast only to re-
appear at the beginning of the ninth still chasing it to no
avail. Wearied and frustrated by his failure, he comes upon
some shepherds whose pleasant and carefree existence so
attracts him that he decides to join them and forsake his
quest. He also chooses to remain in pastoral because of his
attraction to the beautiful Pastorella, and, to court his new
love more successfully, he assumes the guise of a shepherd.
One day during his pastoral interlude, wandering forth
alone, Calidore comes upon Mount Acidale, a hill of in-
credible beauty, sacred to Venus and the muses. There, at
that very moment, the piper Colin Clout is experiencing
an extraordinary vision. Dancing to the music of his pipe
are a "hundred naked maidens lilly white" circling the three
Graces who themselves surround "another Damzell" out-
shining all in loveliness and grace. Enthralled by "the beauty
of this goodly band," Calidore tries to draw nearer only to
make them all vanish, leaving Colin so bereft that he breaks
his pipe. After due apologies for his intrusion, Calidore is
given an explanation of the vision and, enraptured by Colin's
schooling, he wants to stay. But his love for Pastorella draws
him away; Mount Acidale and the piper disappear; Cali-
dore's sojourn is soon disrupted by brigands who destroy
the pastoral idyll and kidnap his beloved. Forced, as a result,
to resume his active life, he eventually rescues Pastorella
from the brigands and then goes on to overcome the Blatant
Beast. By capturing the monster he fulfills his mission and
rightfully wins acclaim as his society's courteous redeemer.

My summary of the hero's adventures deliberately em-
phasizes his pastoral sojourn and his encounter on Mount
Acidale (Cantos ix and x) to convey the impression Spenser
gives us, without explicitly saying so, that these experiences
are necessary for Calidore's courtesy to reach its full po-
tential. Most readers have recognized that Calidore's en-

counter with Colin Clout constitutes the "allegorical core" of Book VI, even though the author deliberately underplays (for reasons I will return to) its central importance. In terms of the narrative design the episode is a digression within a larger digression. And the digressiveness is thematic as well as structural. For Calidore's pastoral sojourn is shown to be an act of truancy, an abdication of his quest and of his civic responsibility. The truancy is also shown to result in the destruction of the pastoral: when the knight of courtesy decides to forsake his public duty and become a shepherd, then no force of order remains to prevent the evil forces of society, embodied in the brigands, from wreaking the havoc that overtakes the green world. On the other hand, the truancy Calidore commits for the sake of love seems necessary for the eventual fulfillment of his public virtue. And as the pastoral experience changed him, the poetic vision of Colin Clout works upon the hero's mind to transform him into a fully realized agent of courtesy. Such fulfillment is largely indicated by his subsequent ability to confront and subdue the Blatant Beast, a feat he was incapable of before his pastoral experience.

What occurs during his adventure on Mount Acidale to bring about this development? The episode, as several commentators have pointed out, allegorizes Spenser's poetics.[2] In the course of it the reader is given a reenactment of the

[2] After all the recent commentary Book VI, Canto x has provoked, I am reluctant to burden it with more interpretation. For some of my remarks, however, I am indebted to previous studies of Book VI. The following ones have been particularly useful, and they should be consulted for more detailed analysis of this episode: Harry Berger, Jr., "A Secret Discipline: *The Faerie Queene*, Book VI," in *Form and Convention in the Poetry of Edmund Spenser*, ed. William Nelson (New York, 1961), pp. 35-75; E. W. Tayler, *Nature and Art in Renaissance Literature* (New York, 1961), pp. 102-120; R. F. Hill, "Colin Clout's Courtesy," *MLR*, 57 (1962), 492-503; William Nestrick, "The Virtuous and Gentle Discipline of Gentlemen and Poets," *ELH* 29 (1962), 357-371; Humphrey Tonkin, *Spenser's Courteous Pastoral* (Oxford, 1972), esp. pp. 124-142, 226-264. I have also benefited from Richard Neuse's "Book VI as Conclusion to *The Faerie Queene*," *ELH* 35 (1968), 329-353, though I disagree with his pessimistic interpretation.

poetic process initially described in the Proem. For the place
where Calidore sees the piper and the vision—"a place,
whose pleasaunce did appere / To pass all others, on the
earth which were" (VI. X. 5-9)—seems to be an image of the
"silver Bowre . . . hidden from view of men" referred to in
the Proem as "the sacred noursery of virtue." And in this
secret place we are shown along with Calidore how the
poet, figured by Colin Clout, is granted access to ideal forms
of virtue when inspired by the muses and by love. The
parallels between the Proem and the scene on Acidale sug-
gest Calidore has not only come upon a poem in the making,
but one that could turn into the poem we actually read.
Indeed, the extraordinary dance envisioned by Colin could
be taken to symbolize the essence of Courtesy as it manifests
itself to the poet alone before he communicates his higher
insight to other men by his mediation. More generally the
dance represents poetic vision in transcendent form, still so
intensely personal that it cannot withstand the presence of
an audience. It therefore disappears upon Calidore's intru-
sion. Yet the hero partakes of it sufficiently and has enough
of it explained by the seer to be decisively illuminated,
eventually transformed.

About the Three Graces figuring in the dance we learn
with Calidore that they bestow whatever comeliness men
display in their activities:

> These three on men all gracious gifts bestow,
>   Which decke the body or adorne the mynde,
>   To make them louely or well fauoured show,
>   As comely carriage, entertainement kynde,
>   Sweete semblaunt, friendly offices that bynde,
>   And all the complements of curtesie:
>   They teach vs, how to each degree and kynde,
>   We should our selues demeane, to low, to hie;
> To friends, to foes, which skill men call Ciuility.
>   (VI. X. 23)

By so ascribing the origin of all beauty in human action to
the Graces, Spenser wants to emphasize that poetry and

courtesy come from the same source, that there is little difference between them. "To Spenser, in fact, as to Shelley or Plato," C. S. Lewis remarked when commenting on the stanza above, "there is no essential difference between poetic beauty and the beauty of characters, institutions, and behaviour, and all alike come from the 'daughters of sky-ruling Jove.'" Like courtesy, poetry is characterized by grace, proportion, and decorum. In both, nature is perfected and disciplined by art and, as manifestations of "disciplynd" Nature, both are acts and forces of order in the world. Colin's own poetic apotheosis of his beloved reminds us that both, moreover, require selflessness and love. Spenser gradually makes us realize that both are intimately linked because courtesy, as he conceives it, is the poetry of conduct.[3] But the poet, Spenser also wants to indicate, enjoys a special communion with the heavenly source from which grace and beauty originate. He serves as the mediator between the Graces and mankind. Not only is his art graced with "the complements of curtesie," but his privileged understanding of their source also allows him to teach men these "complements" so that their conduct, too, can become a poetic achievement. The relation of the Graces to Colin Clout offers a further parallel between Canto x and the Proem for, like the Muses originally invoked, the Graces haunting Mount Acidale (their very haunt reminds one of "Parnasso") reveal to the poet the mysteries that he alone can communicate to other men.

Beneath the guise of mythology Spenser can be seen radically modifying the assumptions that had governed Puttenham's *Arte of English Poesie*. There, too, was expressed the belief that the same principles that constitute beauty in human conduct serve to beautify poetic art. But

[3] For C. S. Lewis' remarks on Spenser's conceptions of courtesy as "the poetry of conduct" see *The Allegory of Love* (New York, 1958), p. 351. Further analogies between Spenser's (and Colin Clout's) poetic conduct and the idea of courtesy in Book vi have been drawn by William Nestrick in "The Virtuous and Gentle Discipline of Gentlemen and Poets," cited in the previous note.

whereas Puttenham assumed that the courtier's becoming
conduct could determine the poet's esthetic standards, Spen-
ser now discloses that the roles have been reversed. Spenser
continues to depict courteous conduct as an essentially
poetic phenomenon, but such a conception of behavior is
precisely what makes him affirm that the poet is uniquely
endowed to understand as well as to teach courtesy. His
breeding notwithstanding, the courtier cannot possess the
acute knowledge of courtesy that the poet, by vocation, has
come to master. He must therefore rely on the poet to
acquire some of that mastery. Spenser reveals the courtier's
dependence on the poet's "gracious gifts" by presenting
Calidore's encounter with Colin Clout as a rite of initiation.
The poet has become the high priest of Courtesy. It is under
his inspired guidance that the courtier as acolyte can be
initiated into its mysteries.

Yet, in order for the knowledge vouchsafed by the poet
to become virtuous action, the hero's recreation must end.
Spenser knows that if someone like Calidore, whose respon-
sibilities lie elsewhere, becomes too attracted to the Muses
and loses himself in the remoteness of pastoral, then society
will become increasingly prone to the devastations of For-
tune. This is the moral implication behind the eruption of
the brigands and the sudden destruction of the green world.
Spenser himself is confronted with a similar dilemma as a
poet. He recognizes that his visionary insight and eloquence
must serve to edify the morals of his community, even while
he knows that poetic inspiration comes to him in the sylvan
privacy of pastoral. No more than Calidore can disregard
his public duty can Spenser ignore the claims that society
makes on his imagination. The pastoral world must be
abandoned, even destroyed. Yet Spenser still indicates that
Calidore's sojourn there was necessary. Through love and
through Colin's intermediacy Calidore has been granted an
idea of human existence poetically fulfilled. Such knowledge
inspires him to improve actual existence upon his return to
it. The overcoming of the brigands and the eventual (if only
temporary) subjugation of the Blatant Beast can be seen as
the knight's attempts to rid society of its imperfections so

that it can regain some of the divine order he had perceived on Acidale. Though Spenser does not state it explicitly, his sequence of events in the last three cantos suggests that Calidore's restoration of social harmony is related to his previous glimpse of its transcendent form. The last canto does not end, however, once Calidore's mission has been accomplished. Just as Spenser will not allow the knight to lose himself in the delights of pastoral, so he won't allow the reader to remain engrossed in his poetic fiction. Like his hero, the reader must be made to move on from recreation to responsibility. By bringing him back in the last two stanzas to a harsh and present actuality, afflicted, once again, by the Blatant Beast, Spenser acknowledges the limits of his poetry but not its inability to work on the reader's will. The very example of his hero's inspired return to the epic world of strife after his encounter with Colin Clout beckons the reader to take back and make use of Spenser's poetic images in his actual life. At least Spenser hopes that, as Calidore moves on from pastoral to act upon the insight he has been granted there, some readers, by using his vision to guide their moral action, can improve themselves and the "degendered" world they inhabit.

The Neoplatonic poetics allegorized in Book VI resemble to a remarkable degree those enunciated at the start of Sidney's *Apology for Poetry*. On Mount Acidale we witness with Calidore how the poet "lifted up with the vigor of his own invention, doth grow in effect into another nature; in making things either better than Nature bringeth forth, or quite anew. . . ." Colin's vision attests, moreover, that "with the force of a divine breath" the poet can reconstitute images of the harmony man has lost by the Fall. For he possesses the "erected wit [that] maketh us know what perfection is" and that can prompt man to reach unto it in spite of his "infected will." By his unique capacity to give beautiful form to the good, he can persuade men "to take that goodness in hande, which without delight they would fly as from a stranger."[4] Indeed, by stirring Calidore to recap-

[4] Sidney, *An Apology for Poetry*, ed. cit., pp. 100-103.

ture its perfect order, Colin's vision serves what Sidney con-
sidered the final and most important end of the learning
poetry so effectively provides: "to lead and draw us to as
high a perfection as our degenerate soules, made worse by
their clayey lodgings are capable of." Both Spenser and Sid-
ney believe that the poet is able to create a world not only
superior to the actual world but capable of shaping and
improving the everyday world men inhabit. Like his prede-
cessor, Spenser seeks to accord the poet a preeminent role
in redeeming society. Yet the basic difference in Spenser's
manner of advancing his claims cannot be overlooked.

Sidney, having composed an oration in defense of poetry,
openly declares that society can be reformed, even re-
deemed, by the poet's god-given talents. Spenser's similar
proposal, however, is left to be inferred. His use of pastoral
romance as a vehicle to allegorize the poet's role obviously
shows he had no intent to assert it directly. But he did not
choose to allegorize it merely for the sake of being indirect.
His covert means serve a number of other motives prompted
by the subject of Book VI. Besides his large claims about
poetry's function, Spenser discloses beneath the veil of his
fiction that the courtier can only perfect his courtesy after
being disciple to a poet. Despite the deteriorated state of
courtly manners, this is not a truth he can easily proclaim.
To maintain that the poet has assumed authority as society's
maker of manners calls for his utmost discretion, since such
a claim, I have already suggested, virtually deprives the
ruling class of one of its cherished prerogatives.

Already in the Proem to Book VI, sensing that his declared
intent to restore an ideal of courtesy might appear pre-
sumptuous, he qualifies it by praising his queen and her
circle as paragons of the virtue. The same tactful deference
to his sovereign reemerges at the moment in his narrative
when the powers of the poet are most fully affirmed: during
Colin's apotheosis of his mistress on Mt. Acidale, or rather
immediately after it. When the vision has vanished, Colin
explains to Calidore that his beloved, though "but a countrey
lass," was the central figure of the extraordinary dance, that

she, elevated by his inspired music, was the object of the celebration. The explanation itself consists of a splendid praise of the girl (VI. X. 25-27), but then the piper becomes concerned lest the extravagant compliment he pays her might be misconstrued as an insult to the queen, supposedly the poet's chief object of praise. So turning to his sovereign, Colin apologizes (and his voice here seems to blend with Spenser's) for allowing the maiden to usurp her majesty's rightful place:

> Great *Gloriana*, greatest Maiesty,
> Pardon thy shepheard, mongst so many layes,
> As he hath sung of thee in all his dayes,
> To make one minime of thy poor handmayd
> And underneathe they feete to place her prayse,
> That when thy glory shall be farre displayd
> To future age of her this mention may be made.
>
> (VI. X. 28)

By reasserting his queen's superiority to the humble subject he has just elevated, the poet indirectly bestows on the monarch the praise lavished on his mistress. It is only because of the queen's glory, he maintains, that her handmaid can hope to share some of her eternal fame. Ironically, the poet's disclaimers, his very need to display such deference, serve to reaffirm his unique power to elevate whomever he deems worthy by poetic praise. But, ostensibly, the aim of this tactful bow is to diminish the evidence, too manifest in the apotheosis of the girl, that he can immortalize the most humble person by the power of his verse. In the Proem, discretion prompted Spenser to temper the large claim he made about his privileged insight as a poet. Here, the same sense of tact makes him attenuate the poetic powers actually demonstrated in the celebration of his beloved.

The tact governing Spenser's occasional flattery is more broadly displayed in the general conduct of his narrative. Does it not seem odd that Colin's vision on Mt. Acidale and his exchange with Calidore, the episode most readers recognize to be the most significant in Book VI, should be so "buried" in the narrative as to appear unimportant? Discretion, however, rather than oddity prompted the author to make this scene a digression within the larger digression of the pastoral interlude. Again, it is because he sought to obfuscate the social statement embodied in the episode that he resorted to such narrative indirection. By making the episode occur in rustic remoteness, he was able to further understate his case. For the cloak of pastoral simplicity offered him the most appropriate literary means of veiling the claims of his poetic manifesto. With a figure so humble and homely as Colin Clout serving as his spokesman, who could accuse Spenser of presumption? Of course, the reader familiar with pastoral conventions would know, as Puttenham did, that "under the vaile of homely persons" the poet meant "to insinuate and glaunce at greater matters." And just to be sure that "greater matters" will be inferred, Spenser offers some telling clues. The deliberate heightening of the verse describing Colin's extraordinary vision, the vision itself, signal the discrepancy between the shepherd's low station and the momentous significance of his activity. Moreover, the polite restraint and civility Colin shows after Calidore's rather boorish intrusion subtly indicate that despite his inferior rank the shepherd-poet possesses more courtesy than its titular hero. Still, Spenser never openly asserts that the poet is better versed in courtesy than the courtier. The traditional humble setting and personages of pastoral allow him to express this truth—which plainly stated might seem impudent—in quite unassuming fashion.

The poet's display of such devious tactics at the very moment the matter of his narrative praises the virtues of rustic life untrammelled by artifice is, itself, a traditional paradox of pastoral poetry.[5] Nor is it the only discrepancy

[5] As others have before him, E. W. Tayler points out that pastoral literature, "no matter what its pretensions to simplicity of form or matter, proves on inspection to be highly stylized and carefully calculated. The reason is simple. Bucolic fiction requires before all else a poet and audience sufficiently civilized to appreciate primitive simplicity, to recognize that the gain of Art means the loss of Nature. To

between the manner and the matter of Spenser's pastoral interlude. Simplicity pretends to reign in the world of Cantos ix and x, but the amorous conduct practiced there proves to be surprisingly sophisticated. And in a setting that passes off as natural, one recognizes, especially when the surpassing beauty of Mt. Acidale is described (vi. x. 5-7), how much art has gone into its improvement. Colin Clout, I already said, displays extraordinary refinement for a simple rustic. In general, the denizens of Spenser's pastoral are far more courteous than any of the poem's supposedly civilized characters. As such discrepancies become more and more notable—and Spenser wants them to be recognized—so do the artistry and sophistication of the author. In fact, the stylistic refinement Spenser displays in veiling his dream of civilization beneath a rustic garb calls attention, in turn, to a broader contradiction in Book vi.

Consider the moral thrust of Spenser's argument as he defines courtesy. "Vertues seat," he claims in the Proem, "is deepe within the mynd / And not in outward shows, but inward thoughts defynd." The couplet well sums up the didactic message of the Sixth Book. To make his readers dissociate courtesy from the outward shows of courtly etiquette and the privileges of being a courtier, Spenser presents the most courteous characters in Book vi—Tristram, the Salvage Man, the Hermit, Pastorella, and Colin Clout—as individuals totally removed from court, dispossessed of social rank, or of low degree. Not that Spenser lacks a strong aristocratic bias: all these characters, except for Colin Clout, turn out to be nobly born, and their gentle manners are shown to be an expression of their gentle blood. Indeed, by stressing the idea that "blood will tell," the author means to emphasize the inborn, natural qualities of

---

regard pastoral literature as simple stuff because it sings of simple things is to confuse the symbol with the thing symbolized. After all, nostalgia for natural simplicity is a sentiment denied those who have experienced only natural simplicity." *Nature and Art in Renaissance Literature* (New York, 1961), p. 5.

courtesy: it can be enhanced by nurture and courtly train-
ing, but an overlay of good manners will not make cour-
teous those who lack the seed of virtue implanted by nature.
Calidore may be a courtier versed in the rules of polite
etiquette, but from the start we are told that his "Gentle-
nesse of spright and manners mylde were planted naturall."
In the course of the narrative we learn with him that cour-
tesy that does not originate from within but consists simply
of external trappings is "nought but forgerie." And during
his pastoral sojourn to prove his own inner worth and
thereby win Pastorella's love, he must discard his outer
"courteous guize" and exercise instead the inborn grace he
naturally possesses. On Mt. Acidale he further learns from
Colin Clout how deep within the mind courtesy resides.
It is because of the inward growth love stimulates, because
of the insight vouchsafed by the poet that Calidore can
finally emerge as a more legitimate champion of courtesy.
Spenser's insistence on the inner sources of the virtue equally
affects his image of the poet and the role ascribed to him in
Book VI. Unsurprisingly, the poet, teacher of courtesy, is
defined in terms of his inner gifts. Cast in the role of moral
reformer, he is a man not only uniquely endowed with
vision but capable of stimulating insight in others, of trans-
forming men's souls. Just as courtesy is "deep within the
mynd, and not in outward shows defynd," so the poet's
ability to inspire it must come from the effects he can exert
upon this inner seat of virtue, not from the example of his
style, the outer garment of his art. Because of Spenser's
emphasis on the interiority of all that has worth, the stylistic
attributes that would also justify the poet's authority as a
teacher of manners appear negligible. So the matter of Spen-
ser's fiction would suggest.

Yet the manner of the poetry goes some way to contra-
dict it. Spenser reveals by the conduct of his narrative, by
his skills as an allegorist, by his tact and his subterfuge, a
total command of the "courteous guizes" he ostensibly dis-
credits. Despite his criticism of the superficial and rhetorical
aspects of courtesy, the cunning that graces his art reveals

that he still cherishes beautiful style enough not to disregard "outward shows" altogether. Spenser knows too that the aristocracy asserts its social eminence by refined comportment and stylistic mastery. To be acknowledged by his courtly readers as a maker of manners, the poet must prove his stylistic proficiency, even more perhaps than his moral authority. The subtlety with which he presents his argument in Book VI becomes such a demonstration of the poet's refinement. I would maintain that the discretion, the indirection, even the dissimulation he so impressively exercises are themselves proof of the poet's proclaimed authority as an arbiter of manners. No sophisticated courtly reader could dismiss him for stylistic deficiency after appreciating the subtlety and delightful cunning he displays in advancing his claim. In fact the mastery of tact and indirection Spenser displays in his verbal manners does more than remove any doubts about his stylistic expertise. It serves to demonstrate his ability to outshine any "cunning Princepleaser" in the art of feigning and thereby affirms that he is indeed qualified to give courtiers lessons in graceful comportment.

The discrepancy between the poetic matter and manner in Book VI does not diminish Spenser's reservations about "outward shows" and men's manipulations of their external selves. Nonetheless, the cunning and artifice gracing his poetry show that, for all his emphasis on the natural and interior sources of courtesy, he still values the art by which courtesy is made externally becoming. His profound misgivings about surface appearances must not obscure his belief (natural for a poet) that the neglect of external comeliness can be as reproachable as moral turpitude. He may deplore artifice that cloaks emptiness and malice within, but his own verbal manners in Book VI serve as proof that deceptive artifice is not always sinister.[6] They indicate, on the contrary, that outward guises can be commendable—as long as these guises veil inner worth. Beautiful courtiers had been

[6] For a fine account of Spenser's ambivalent attitudes to artifice in the epic as a whole see Hans Guth, "Allegorical Implications of Artifice in Spenser's *Faerie Queene*," *PMLA* 76 (1961), 474-479.

supposed to exemplify how cunning could be so used in the
service of communicating moral truth. But now that "beau-
tie and good grace" more often serve to mask "vile treason
and fowle falsehood" (IV. I. 17), the poet emerges as the
one legitimate practitioner of salutary deception. If men are
to regain the art of giving truth beautiful guises—and this
remains desirable in beautiful conduct—they must model
themselves on the poet's exemplary artifices. That is what
Spenser finally wants his readers to infer from his masterly
use of "fained colors shading a true case."

It should be said that as much as the stylistic refinement
and exemplary artifice Spenser displays in Book VI serve to
confirm his authority as a legislator of beautiful conduct,
these skills remain subordinate to the poet's chief claim for
that authority: his privileged insight of higher truths. How-
ever impressive his beautiful cunning, it seems that he wants
it to be considered as the lesser part of his talent. Of course
the impression he gives the reader that his ability "to in-
sinuate and glaunce at greater matters" is almost incidental
could be taken as a deliberate act of *sprezzatura*, intended
as further proof of his sophistication. Yet Spenser has
another motive for so underplaying his rhetorical virtuosity.
In the last finished book of his epic Spenser does not merely
want to show that the poet outshines the courtier in comely
manners. He seeks, above all, to establish the uniqueness of
the poet's social role. And proficient though the poet may
be in matters of style, such expertise does not make him
unique. Courtiers and other civilized men can share his
stylistic mastery—if need be by modelling themselves on
his example. The talents, however, that really warrant his
authority as a maker of manners—his power of insight, the
privileged inspiration he is granted from above—these be-
long exclusively to the poet. Certainly no courtier can
possess them. The latter may benefit from the poet's god-
given attributes, but he cannot share them. By insisting on
the poet's visionary powers rather than on his rhetorical
skills, Spenser ultimately so aggrandizes his social function
that it is no longer possible to identify his art with the

courtier's, even though the ties between them are not yet
severed.

The ties between them have not been severed, but they
are radically altered nevertheless—that remains the most re-
markable aspect of Book VI in the light of the preceding
history. Spenser has reversed the assumptions that governed
Puttenham's *Arte of English Poesie*: the poet can help im-
prove the courtier's conduct rather than the other way
around. From having been a model of comportment for the
poet to imitate, the courtier is now asked to become the
poet's disciple. In reversing rather than severing the ties
between poet and courtier, Spenser reveals, incidentally,
that his anti-courtly sentiments remained ambivalent to the
end. He may challenge the prerogative of the "great" to
dictate standards of courtesy, but the very hope he expresses
of improving their comportment shows a continuing faith
in their virtuous capacity. Even though he proposes that the
poet must assume the task of inspiring better conduct among
those who rule England, he does not abandon the notion that
the courtly aristocracy can regain the exemplary role it
should set for society. To be sure, he has lost faith in the
ability of courtiers to restore, by their own effort, the art
of conduct they currently debase. In fact, while lamenting
the courtiers' failure to live up to their image as society's
makers of manners, Spenser exploits that failure to strength-
en his claims about the poet's unique ability to set a pattern
of courtesy for the nation.

᳄

From a broader historical perspective Spenser's image
of the poet as a legislator of manners hardly seems new.
The conception of the poet as a civilizing agent, a founder
of society, and a teacher of manners had served, since early
antiquity, to justify the value of his art. Throughout the
Renaissance one finds poetry's supporters invoking the stories
of Orpheus and Amphion (following Horace's example in
the *Ars Poetica*, 391-403) to assert the poet's power of re-

forming men and institutions. So, for instance, Puttenham
remarks at the beginning of his *Arte* that *"Orpheus* assem-
bled the wild beastes to come in heards to harken his musicke,
and by that means made them tame, implying thereby how
by his discrete and wholsome lessons uttered in harmonie
and with melodious instruments, he brought the rude and
savage people to a more civill and orderly life" (p. 6). Be-
sides Orpheus and Amphion writers pointed to Homer and
Virgil, especially the latter's ethical and political teaching
in the *Aeneid*, to affirm the poet's educational and civilizing
role. Of course, English Renaissance poets could only claim
that they were fulfilling such a dignified role when their
own achievement had grown comparable to the poetic
legacy of antiquity. Usually it is Ben Jonson and not Spen-
ser who is credited with having actively promoted the idea
that the contemporary poet was society's preeminent arbiter
of manners. Jonson receives more credit for it primarily
because he states the idea in the most forthright way. "A
teacher of things divine no less than human, a master in
manners," he calls the poet in the Epistle to "The Two
Famous Universities" prefacing *Volpone*. And in *Timber*,
or Discoveries he unabashedly proposes that the poet, by
virtue of his authority on esthetic, ethical, and political
matters, is supremely qualified to counsel the ruling class
about its moral and social responsibilities. "I could never
thinke," he writes,

> the study of *Wisdome* confin'd only to the Philosopher:
> or of *Piety* to the Divine: or of *State* to the Politicke. But
> that he which can faine a *Common-wealth* (which is the
> *Poet*) can governe it with *Counsels*, strengthen it with
> *Lawes*, correct it with *Judgements*, informe it with *Re-*
> *ligion*, and *Morals*; is all these. Wee doe not require in
> him meere *Elocution*; or an excellent faculty in verse; but
> the exact knowledge of all vertues, and their Contraries;
> with ability to render the one lov'd, the other hated, by
> his proper embattaling them.[7]

[7] *Ben Jonson*, ed. C. H. Herford, Percy and Evelyn Simpson (Ox-
ford, 1947), VIII, p. 595. For some valuable comments on Jonson's

Spenser had said as much in *The Faerie Queene*, only less directly. And before Jonson suggested it in *Timber*, he had already proposed that, since virtuous conduct was essentially poetic, poets were therefore preeminently qualified to understand and teach men proper manners. But Spenser could not lecture his social superiors about their comportment as overtly as did Jonson in his verse epistles, and not just because one poet was more subservient than the other. At the time Spenser was advancing his claims about the poet, the moral and social authority of the English aristocracy had not yet drastically eroded. The Elizabethan poet still had to vie with that authority. In the process of claiming that he was more of a "master in manners" than the Elizabethan courtier, he had to prove it by outshining the latter in grace. The indirection, the tact, the modest guise of the shepherd-poet were among Spenser's means, as we saw, of establishing this superiority. He was more oblique, less assertive than Jonson in advancing the poet's social authority partly because such indirection helped to enforce his claims. Spenser, I am proposing, was as responsible as Jonson—but a generation earlier—for enhancing the identity of the poet in England. However, to understand why he could not be as forthright about it as his successor, one needs to take into account the history of poetry and courtliness previously sketched.

I want to emphasize in closing that, though claims for the poet's social and moral authority have a long tradition, they could not be made in Elizabethan England before the poet felt secure enough about his identity to present himself as more qualified to legislate beautiful manners than the courtier, the individual who had been entrusted by Elizabethans to fulfill that role. When Spenser composed Book VI, he

conception of the poet's social role as it is expressed in his poems and his critical prose see Hugh Maclean, "Ben Jonson's Poems: Notes on the Ordered Society," reprinted in *Seventeenth Century Poetry*, ed. William R. Keast (New York, 1971), pp. 174-200.

possessed that self-confidence. Moreover, changing attitudes in the last decade of Elizabeth's reign—specifically the declining faith in the courtier's social authority—allowed him to give his argument about the poet's unique civilizing function an immediacy it would otherwise lack. He made the traditional conception of the poet as an arbiter of conduct more credible to his contemporaries, and more vital an issue, by taking advantage of the courtier's loss of eminence as such an arbiter. In doing so he points to a final irony in the history of poetry and courtliness as I have traced it. The cultivation of proper court style as well as the vitality of the myth of the perfect courtier in Elizabethan England benefited the development of English poetry. But it should now be also evident that the decline of this myth, the growing disaffection with courtly manners as actually practiced, served equally to advance the status of poetry. The poet shared, as we saw, many attributes with the model courtier. It was because of such affinities that his art proved so congenial to courtly taste and acquired greater respectability. So, because of such affinities, when courtiers ceased to win Englishmen's admiration as civilized and civilizing agents, the poet's art could assume the function they had not fulfilled. Men had proved unable to be like poems, but some gifted men continued to create poems. Just as their art had benefited from its associations with proper courtliness, so poets gained from the loss of faith in model conduct at court. For the absence of perfect courtiers left the poet as society's most prominent agent of beautiful manners and morals. And, as Spenser shows, he could actually take advantage of the courtier's loss of that role to reassert all the more forcefully the poet's traditional function of civilizing mankind. In the end, then, the decline of the myth of the perfect courtier helped the English Renaissance poet as the rise of the myth had helped him. For in the course of its decline it prompted the revival of another, more lasting myth that had always been of service to poets: that society can be saved by their art.

Index

anti-courtly sentiments, 111, 113, 131; Elizabethan, 119-24, 132; in Spenser's poetry, 123, 124, 132-35, 137, 138, 143-44, 159

Aristotle, 42; *Rhetoric*, 117

Ascham, Roger, *The Schole-master*, 121-23

Augustine, St., 108n

Baldwin, T. W., 7n, 8

Baron, Hans, 12n

Baxandall, Michael, 19n, 48

Berger, Harry, Jr., 93n, 147n

Blunt, Sir Charles, 71n

Burckhardt, Jacob, 12n, 42n

Burke, Kenneth, 61n, 84

Castiglione, Baldassare, 15, 68, 75, 105, 107, 117, 118, 124; *The Book of the Courtier*, 4, 10, 18, 54, 55-61, 67, 69, 74, 86-87, 88, 92-97, 121, 122, 123, 124; compared to Cicero's *De oratore*, 23-49; influence in Tudor England, 4-5, 18n, 55, 121, 131-32

Cecil, Robert, 126, 127, 129

Cecil, William, Lord Burghley, 126, 127, 129n

Chapman, George, 65

Cicero, 14, 20, 117; *Brutus*, 21; *De oratore*, 18, 21-49 *passim*, 61; *Orator*, 21

clarity, as a rhetorical norm, 37, 38, 61, 64-66, 77

Clark, D. L., 8

courtesy, 141-48, 155-56; poet as master of, 16-17, 139-40, 149-50, 152, 154, 157-62

Cyvile and Uncyvile Life, 5n

Davis, Walter, 94

Day, Angel, 62n, 64

deceit, *see* deception, dissimulation

deception, necessary at court, 46, 117; salutary, 44-45, 95-96, 118, 158; Spenser's concern with, 133-37, 139-40, 157-58. *See also* dissimulation

decorum, 51-53, 144-45

despotism, 9-11, 12n, 14, 46-49; and courtly behavior, 27, 46, 117-18

didacticism, court's low toler-ance of, 30, 44-45, 86, 95-96, 98, 99; made pleasurable by poet, 96-101, 105-106

dissimulation, 111-12, 114, 117; and courtly grace, 36, 55-58; distinguished from deceit and fraud, 57, 67-68, 110, 157-58; esteemed at court, 38, 66, 90; hostility towards, 108-10, 131; poetic, 58-64 *passim*, 67, 78-86, 90, 157

Donne, John, 84n, 117n, 132

Edwards, Thomas, 135n

Elizabeth I, Queen, 16, 67, 68, 71, 73, 120, 127, 128, 129, 130; Spenser's praise of, 133, 134, 143-45, 153;
    Court of: 3, 4, 5, 15, 54, 69-74, 119, 137-38; corruption at, 127-30; criticized, 113, 121-22, 123, 133-34, 143; declining re-spect for, 125, 130, 131-32, 138, 162; praised, 69, 120-21

elocutio, 37, 65, 77, 85. *See also* ornament

emblems, 79, 80n

Empson, William, 82

Erasmus, Desiderius, 11n, 48n, 117

Library of Congress Cataloging in Publication Data

Javitch, Daniel.
    Poetry and courtliness in Renaissance England.

    Includes index.
    1. English poetry—Early modern, 1500-1700—History
and criticism.   2. Great Britain—Court and courtiers.
3. Literature and society.   I. Title.
    PR535.C69J3   821'.009   77-85541
    ISBN 0-691-06354-0